Women in Vanuatu

Women in Vanuatu

*Analyzing Challenges to
Economic Participation*

Chakriya Bowman
Jozefina Cutura
Amanda Ellis
Clare Manuel

THE WORLD BANK
Washington, D.C.

©2009 The International Bank for Reconstruction and Development/The World Bank

1818 H Street, NW
Washington, DC 20433
Telephone: 202-473-1000
Internet: www.worldbank.org
E-mail: feedback@worldbank.org

ISBN: 978-0-8213-7909-7
eISBN: 978-0-8213-7910-3
DOI: 10.1596/978-0-8213-7909-7

Library of Congress Cataloging-in-Publication Data has been applied for.

Cover photo courtesy of the Australian Agency for International Development, copyright Rob Maccoll 2007, the Port Vila vegetable market.
Cover design: Naylor Design.

Contents

Boxes

Figures

Map

Tables

Preface and Acknowledgments

This report is the result of collaboration between the Australian Agency for International Development (AusAID) and the World Bank Group. The report has been produced for:

- *AusAID:* to assist development programs to mainstream gender and to enable women to benefit equitably from improvements in the business climate.
- *The World Bank Group:* as a pilot South Pacific contribution to the Doing Business Gender Project. The project is a two-year research program aimed at identifying and analyzing laws, regulations, and administrative barriers that affect women's ability to participate in private sector development. Focusing on the World Bank's *Doing Business* indicators, the project is also developing an international database of laws and identifying best practice reforms.
- *The International Finance Corporation (IFC):* to inform its Vanuatu Regulatory Simplification and Investment Policy and Promotion Project and ensure that gender issues are incorporated in the project's design and implementation.
- *The government of Vanuatu:* to make recommendations for reform actions for government to further enable women in Vanuatu to participate effectively in the country's economic development.

Research for the report was primarily carried out during a mission to Vanuatu on April 21–25, 2008. The mission team, led by Amanda Ellis (World Bank), included Sonali Bishop (IFC), Kristie Drucza (AusAID), Anna Hutchins (Australian National University), Clare Manuel (The Law & Development Partnership), and Vijaya Nagarajan (Macquarie University). Jozefina Cutura (World Bank consultant) and Kristie Drucza (AusAID) undertook useful preparatory research on March 3–7, 2008.

The authors wish to thank all the individuals who provided us with helpful information and were available for interviews during the in-country research. They include the Vanuatu government's various ministries and departments, the Vanuatu Investment Promotion Agency (VIPA), donors, the Chamber of Commerce, VANWODS, and the banking institutions. We also thank the National Council of Women for its valuable insights into the overall position of women in Vanuatu's society.

We are especially grateful to the AusAID mission, and notably Anna Naupa of AusAID Vanuatu, for the exceptional organization and support she provided during the mission and for generously sharing her valuable insights and knowledge.

Finally, we wish to thank the wonderful women entrepreneurs who took the time to share their stories and challenges during focus group discussions in Port Vila and on Santos and Tanna islands.

Foreword

Women's contributions to poverty reduction, economic growth, and private sector development are increasingly recognized globally. A growing amount of research demonstrates the link between women's empowerment and societal well-being. Yet research also indicates that women's economic contributions continue to lag behind their achievements in health and education, and a variety of barriers still prevent women in many parts of the world from fully contributing to the economy.

Cognizant of the need to address this disparity, the World Bank Group initiated a Gender Action Plan in 2007 to promote "Gender Equality as Smart Economics." The plan supports Millennium Development Goal #3 by advancing women's economic empowerment and gender equality over a period of four years throughout the work of the World Bank Group. Generously sponsored by AusAID and produced in collaboration with the Foreign Investment Advisory Service (FIAS) and the International Finance Corporation (IFC) Sydney Office, this publication has been produced under the auspices of the Gender Action Plan and its continued efforts to better integrate gender concerns into private sector development programs.

Women in Vanuatu are crucial contributors to society and perceived as those who hold families and communities together. There is a strong emphasis on their role as nurturers and protectors of culture, as well as an association with religious worship and motherhood. While women are increasingly entering the formal economic sphere in Vanuatu, their potential is hindered by a number of barriers and the institutional, legal, and regulatory environment that continues to disadvantage them. The lack of in-depth research on the subject has meant that these obstacles have not been fully examined or addressed to date.

Women in Vanuatu: Analyzing Challenges to Economic Participation is a step toward filling this gap, spurred by the growing recognition in Vanuatu and the broader Pacific region of the need to better address gender inequalities. The publication presents a comprehensive analysis of institutional, legal, and regulatory barriers to women's full economic participation in Vanuatu and proposes measures to address these to ensure a level playing field for both women and men. This work has been a collaborative effort between AusAID and the World Bank's Gender Group, in partnership with IFC and FIAS. A number of the study's recommendations, which emerged from consultations with representatives of the government, the private sector, and civil society in Vanuatu, are being addressed in World Bank Group regional programming going forward.

The World Bank Group is committed to helping governments improve the business environment in the Pacific region through a comprehensive set of activities. We have been pleased to support this integration of gender issues into our investment climate work and hope that the research and its recommendations will catalyze not only increased attention to the role of women in economic development, but will also ultimately help create a business environment that benefits women and men, families, and communities in Vanuatu.

Nigel Roberts
Country Director
Timor-Leste, Papua New Guinea, and the Pacific Islands
World Bank
Sydney, Australia

Abbreviations

AusAID	Australian Agency for International Development
CEDAW	Convention on the Elimination of All Forms of Discrimination against Women
ESCAP	Economic and Social Commission for Asia and the Pacific (United Nations)
FIC	foreign island country
FLO	Fairtrade Labelling Organizations International
GNI	gross national income
IFC	International Finance Corporation
ILO	International Labor Organization
JICA	Japan International Cooperation Agency
NBV	National Bank of Vanuatu
NGO	nongovernmental organization
NPAW	National Plan of Action for Women
PACER	Pacific Agreement for Closer Economic Relations
UNDP	United Nations Development Programme
VANWODS	Vanuatu Women in Development Scheme
VIPA	Vanuatu Investment Promotion Authority
VT	vatu
WFTO	World Fair Trade Organization
WTO	World Trade Organization

All dollar amounts are U.S. dollars unless otherwise indicated.

Map 1 Vanuatu

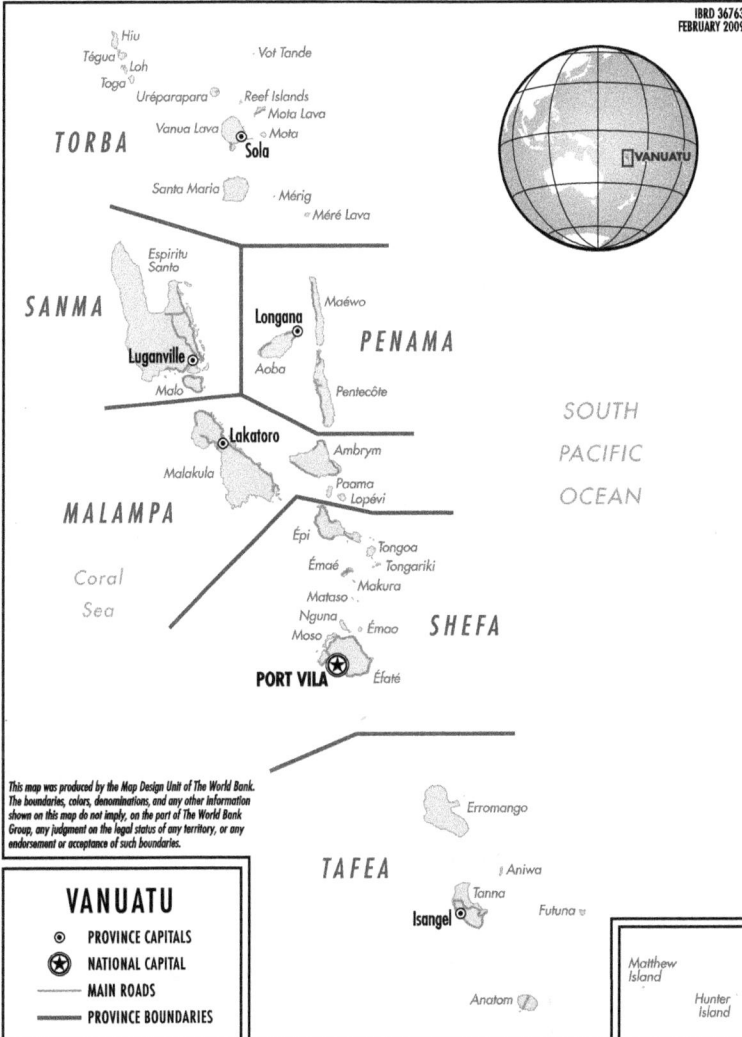

IBRD 36763
FEBRUARY 2009

Hiu
Tégua Loh
Toga
Uréparapara
Vot Tande
Reef Islands
Mota Lava
Vanua Lava Mota
Sola
TORBA
Santa Maria
Mérig
Méré Lava
Espiritu Santo
SANMA
Maéwo
Longana
PENAMA
Luganville
Aoba
Malo
Pentecôte
Lakatoro
Ambrym
Malakula
Paama
Lopévi
MALAMPA
Épi
Coral Sea
Tongoa
Émaé
Tongariki
Makura
Mataso
Nguna
Moso
Émao
SHEFA
PORT VILA
Éfaté
SOUTH PACIFIC OCEAN
Erromango
TAFEA
Aniwa
Tanna
Isangel
Futuna
Matthew Island
Anatom
Hunter Island

VANUATU

- ⊙ PROVINCE CAPITALS
- ✪ NATIONAL CAPITAL
- — MAIN ROADS
- ▬ PROVINCE BOUNDARIES

Overview

Government will continue to pursue policies that will create the necessary environment to attract investment, including much government focus on reducing the cost of doing business.

Honorable Willie Jimmy Tanpangaranuan
Vanuatu Minister of Finance and Economic Management

Introduction

Vanuatu's Government Is Focused on Enabling Economic Growth through Private Sector Development

The government's National Vision for Vanuatu focuses on economic growth led by the private sector and emphasizes the government's role in creating an enabling environment for both domestic and foreign investors. The disadvantaged role of women in society is acknowledged, but the document focuses mainly on gender issues in health, education, and political participation. The *National Plan of Action for Women 2007–2011* includes an explicit focus on women in the economy, promoting women's access to employment, appropriate working conditions, and control over economic resources.[1]

There Is Growing Recognition of the Importance of Gender Issues in Economic Development Matters

World Bank research demonstrates correlations between higher shares of female entrepreneurs and women in the labor force and the ease of doing business (figure 1).

From a development perspective, too, investing in women and gender equality makes sound economic sense. Evidence suggests that developing countries with higher gender equality tend to have lower poverty rates (figure 2).

Figure 1   Greater Ease of Doing Business, More Women Entrepreneurs and Workers

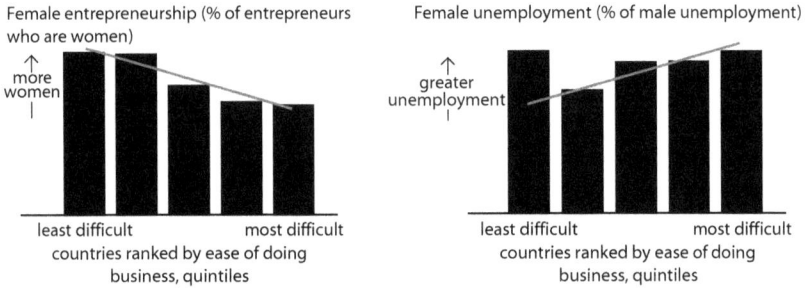

Female entrepreneurship (% of entrepreneurs who are women)

↑ more women

least difficult   most difficult
countries ranked by ease of doing business, quintiles

Female unemployment (% of male unemployment)

↑ greater unemployment

least difficult   most difficult
countries ranked by ease of doing business, quintiles

Source: World Bank 2007.

Figure 2   Poverty and Gender Equality

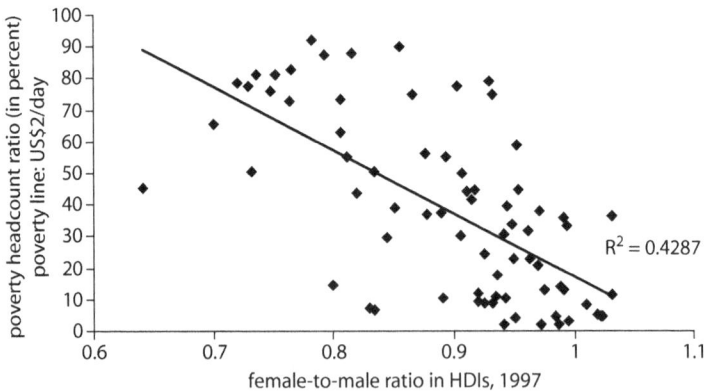

poverty headcount ratio (in percent)
poverty line: US$2/day

$R^2 = 0.4287$

female-to-male ratio in HDIs, 1997

Source: Morrison, Raju, and Sindha 2007.
Note: The scatter plot shows 73 countries. The poverty line is defined as US$2/day. The Human Development Index (HDI) ranks countries globally based on their levels of human development.

There is a strong correlation between women's economic empowerment and economic growth (Verschoor and others 2006). The United Nations Economic and Social Commission for Asia and the Pacific (ESCAP) has estimated that the Asia-Pacific region is losing more than $40 billion per year because of women's limited access to employment, and $16 billion to $30 billion because of gender gaps in education (ESCAP 2007). When women are economically empowered, the benefits flow not only to them but also to their families, communities, and ultimately to the country as a whole (Morrison, Raju, and Sindha 2007; Schultz 2002). Research shows that as women gain control of monetary resources and household budgets, the money spent on education, health, and nutrition increases (Hoddinot and Haddad 1995; Pitt and Khandker 1998; World Bank 2001). Redressing gender inequalities is important in Vanuatu because the country has one of the lowest social indicator rankings in the Pacific.[2]

Creating a Level Playing Field for Women in Business Is Integral to the Government's Priorities of Reducing Poverty and Enabling Economic Growth through Private Sector Development

This report analyzes barriers to women doing business in Vanuatu using the World Bank Group's *Doing Business* indicators as a framework.[3] By analyzing the gender dimensions of the cost of doing business, it considers how to take forward reforms to benefit women as well as men.

Doing Business in Vanuatu

There Are Many Challenges and High Costs Associated with Operating a Business in a Small and Remote Island State

They include:

- Remoteness and isolation resulting in relatively high transport costs, coupled with a small domestic market (Vanuatu's small population of 215,000 is scattered over 65 islands)
- Exposure to events in global markets and trade regimes, over which the country has little influence
- Susceptibility to natural disasters and environmental change
- Limited diversification because of small domestic markets
- Limited capacity in the public and private sector.

Vanuatu's economy has been growing rapidly. Although doing business in Vanuatu is still not easy by international standards, recent reforms have

Figure 3   *Doing Business* Rankings—Vanuatu and Comparator Economies

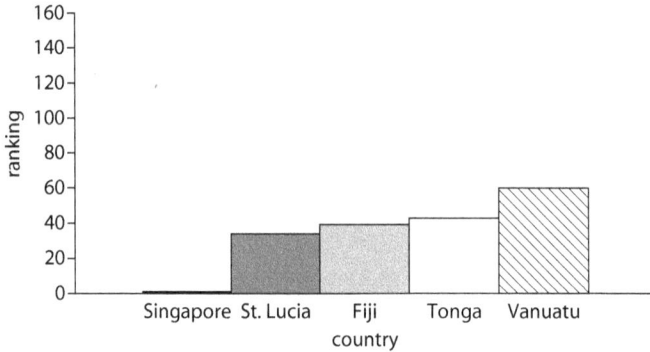

Source: World Bank 2008.

helped improve its international ranking. The country is ranked 60th of 181 economies in the World Bank's *Doing Business in 2009* report, behind several other small island states including Singapore (1st); St Lucia (34th); Fiji (39th); and Tonga (43rd) (figure 3). Three factors—trading across borders (Vanuatu is ranked 136th), registering property (115th), and starting a business (94th) are largely to blame. For women in business, gender issues exacerbate problems.

The government of Vanuatu has recognized the importance of addressing these issues, and is taking forward important legal and regulatory reforms to reduce the costs of doing business (table 1).[4] Vanuatu has recently enacted a new best practice Personal Property Securities Act, is introducing alternative dispute resolution to ease the backlog in the courts, and plans to computerize its land registry. It makes good economic sense to design and implement these measures so that they benefit all businesses in Vanuatu—those run by women as well as by men.

Women in Business in Vanuatu

Vanuatu Is a Traditionally Male-dominated and Largely Patriarchal Society

Women have extremely low rates of participation in Parliament and in other decision-making bodies. Traditional custom law, administered by chiefs and recognized by the Vanuatu Constitution, can operate to discriminate against women (Office of the Prime Minister 2004).

Table 1   Vanuatu—Ranking in the *Doing Business* Index

Ease of....	Doing Business 2009 rank	Doing Business 2008 rank[a]	Change in rank
Doing business	60	67	+7
Starting a business	94	77	−17
Dealing with licenses	24	23	−1
Employing workers	86	86	0
Registering property	115	113	−2
Getting credit	84	126	+42
Protecting investors	70	66	−4
Paying taxes	20	20	0
Trading across borders	136	147	+11
Enforcing contracts	67	67	0
Closing a business	50	52	+2

Source: World Bank 2007; World Bank 2008.
a. *Doing Business* rankings have been recalculated to reflect changes to the methodology and the addition of three new countries. Number 1 is the top ranking.

Despite ratification of the UN Convention on the Elimination of all Forms of Discrimination against Women, a number of Vanuatu's laws continue to discriminate against women, including laws that relate to matrimonial property, inheritance, and citizenship. Domestic violence against women appears to be a serious and growing problem.

As in many other societies, economically active women in Vanuatu suffer from a double workday—combining responsibilities for home and family with their economic activities. Although female enrollment rates are growing faster than male enrollment rates and girls now make up for the first time the majority (52 percent) of those enrolled in secondary education, women remain less likely than men to go on to tertiary education and are less likely to be awarded government scholarships (Vanuatu Rural Development and Training Centers Association 2007).

Nonetheless, Women Are Increasingly Involved in Private Sector Development and in the Market Economy

Sex-disaggregated data on private sector development in Vanuatu are very limited, but the 1999 census suggests that women own nearly 30 percent of all businesses, and, according to a survey by the International Finance Corporation's Pacific Enterprise Development Facility (PEDF 2003), approximately 20 percent of small and medium enterprises. Sixty-four percent of all businesses have between one and nine employees, and over 90 percent of businesses are located in the two major urban centers of Port Vila and Luganville (Vanuatu Statistics Office 2000). The IFC survey suggests that Vanuatu has a low proportion of women-owned microenterprises compared with other countries in the region, but it has one of the highest proportions of women-owned medium-size enterprises.

Government Support for Women's Economic Empowerment and Women in Business Has Been Limited

The Department of Women's Affairs, tasked with implementing the National Plan of Action for Women 2007–2011, has limited capacity and resources, and other ministries such as Finance and Trade are not actively engaged with follow-up.[5] The most visible practical initiative has been VANWODS, a microfinance scheme for women established in 1996 and now run independently. The Department of Cooperatives provides support for women's groups with savings and loans schemes, and the Rural Economic Development Initiative also includes a focus on women in rural areas.

Reforms Are Needed to the General Legal Framework to Ensure Gender Equality

Women in Vanuatu are running their businesses in the context of a legal framework that discriminates against them in some important respects. Although the constitution guarantees nondiscrimination, the extent of the guarantees and their relation to custom law are unclear. Women often do not fare well when using custom law in resolving family law disputes. Moreover, a number of laws that discriminate against women remain on the statute books. To eliminate this discrimination, the following steps are recommended:

- Clarify the relationship between custom and formal law and the apparent contradictions between the two regarding gender equality.
- Ensure better female representation in Parliament and on decision-making bodies, for example by enacting a constitutional requirement for 30 percent female representation on such bodies.
- Ensure that the recently enacted Family Protection Order Bill is implemented to give women proper protection in cases of domestic violence.
- Amend key laws, such as the Matrimonial Causes Act and the Citizenship Act, to end discrimination against women regarding matrimonial property and other gender-related issues.

Starting a Business in Vanuatu Is Costly, Time Consuming, and Disadvantageous to Women

It costs nearly 55 percent of the country's annual per capita income and takes 39 days to start a business in Vanuatu. Most businesses are microenterprises and operate informally or semiformally. There are a number of routes to formalizing a business, the most important of which are formation of companies (under the Companies Act) or cooperatives (under the Cooperative Societies Act). In both cases the processes are lengthy and cumbersome by international standards. Men register many more companies than do women. But women appear to find the cooperative a particularly attractive business form—they make up 30–40 percent of cooperative members.

Although there is no evidence of direct discrimination against women seeking to register their businesses as companies, complex company formation provisions, requiring the assistance of a professional, are likely to be a problem for women, who may be less educated or confident than their male counterparts in dealing with officials. Planned reforms to simplify and streamline Vanuatu's Companies Act are therefore likely to be of particular benefit to women entrepreneurs. Similar streamlining and simplification need to be undertaken in relation to entry procedures under the Cooperative Societies Act.

The requirement for sole traders or partnerships to register under the Business Names Act (unless they are trading under their proprietors' name) is not enforced. Similar regimes in England and Wales and other countries have been perceived as burdensome and abolished. Although Vanuatu's law is not officially enforced, banks may require a business name certificate as a prerequisite to lending.

The business licensing regime operates as a tax, serving no regulatory purpose. The fee must be paid by all businesses, no matter how small, and imposes a significant challenge to microenterprises, many of which are run by women. To ease these difficulties for both women and men, this report offers the following recommendations:

- Streamline the Companies Act in accordance with international best practice, making company formation simpler and abolishing complex and technical legal concepts.
- Streamline the cooperatives regime, so that it imposes no greater regulatory burden than the reformed Companies Act. Consider distinguishing between trading and nontrading cooperatives and tailor the regulation accordingly.

- Abolish the requirement for the registration of business names.
- Review the business licensing regime. Consider abolition, or at least exemption, for microenterprises or a reduction in fees for microentrepreneurs to better reflect their income levels.

Women Own Little Land in Vanuatu and Have Limited Decision-making Rights over Land That Can Be Used for Productive Purposes

Land registration in Vanuatu is extremely problematic. It is a costly and time-consuming process by international standards. Land is a vital economic resource for agriculture and tourism. Vanuatu's land laws do not explicitly discriminate against women, but 97 percent of the land in the country is held under customary tenure (Nari 2000), which generally means that women have very limited rights to control and manage land.

Women's rights over land are increasingly threatened because the rights they do have—to use the land—cannot be registered. Once customary land is registered, women's rights over it tend to be extinguished. The Vanuatu land registry reports that of the 30,000 registered leases, fewer than 20 are in the sole name of a woman (although more are in the joint names of husband and wife). Vanuatu's constitution gives full land ownership to indigenous custom land owners and their descendants (Article 73), but ambiguities are many, and tales of exploitation widespread. The constitution encourages Island Courts to decide matters "wherever possible in conformity with custom." Land inheritance is mainly patrilineal, and while women usually have access and usage rights to land, they do not often have decision-making rights. Women are rarely part of land tribunals, which resolve customary land disputes (21 percent of adjudicators are women) and therefore have limited opportunity to influence decisions in their favor (Office of Prime Minister 2004; Naupa and Simo 2007).

These issues have been recognized by the 2006 National Women's Forum and the National Land Summit, whose recommendations for enhanced and clarified land rights for women are being taken forward by the National Land Steering Committee. Recommendations include:

- Implement the National Land Summit recommendation for research into gender roles relating to land and encourage chiefs to support women's participation in land matters and to promote women's traditional leadership roles.

- Mainstream consultation with women stakeholders in government administration processes relating to land (such as grant of land leases, environmental impact assessments, and infrastructure development).
- Provide more information about and be proactive in ensuring that women's overriding rights to land (such as rights of way, rights to use the land) are registered in the land registry.
- Enhance participation of women on land boards and committees.
- Include in the National Land Steering Committee's public awareness campaign about land reform a campaign educating Vanuatu about the benefits of including women in decision making and the risks to social security when they are marginalized in land matters.

Accessing Finance Is a Constraint for Women

Women in Vanuatu are benefiting from microfinance schemes, but few own land that they can use as collateral for larger loans. Moreover, the absence of a credit reference system means that their repayment histories are not readily accessible and transferable, impeding their access to formal financing. A new personal property secured transactions law has the potential to help women by enabling them to use assets other than land as collateral for loans. Recommendations for increasing access to finance for women include:

- Investigate the potential for a regional credit reference bureau.
- Expedite the implementation of the new Personal Property Secured Transactions Act, and the setting up of the new electronic registry.
- Investigate with commercial banks and finance houses the potential for developing new financial products in response to the new act.
- Undertake outreach programs associated with the new act, especially aimed at women.
- Provide financial literacy training for women bank borrowers.

Women Find It Difficult to Enforce Contracts

In practice the only route to justice open to many women is to rely on chiefs who dispense custom law. The most accessible courts in the formal system are Island Courts, but these also dispense traditional justice. The government should:

- Within the framework of the IFC's alternative dispute resolution procedures, train female mediators and run a public awareness campaign on the benefits of mediation. A component of the campaign should target female entrepreneurs.

Employment Law Discriminates against Women But Is Being Reformed

Most employment in Vanuatu is informal, but women are increasingly entering the formal labor market and now make up about a third of employees. Women's employment tends to be in traditional roles. The law provides for nondiscrimination in the workplace, and maternity and child care provisions are generous. However, the law still includes some discriminatory provisions, such as a prohibition on night work. The new Employment Act Amendment, passed by Parliament in November 2008, still bars women from working at night except under certain conditions and in certain jobs such as nursing and the hospitality industry. We recommend that the government:

• Pass another amendment to the Employment Act to address the night working provisions for women.

The full list of recommendations is summarized in table 2, below, with suggested actions for Vanuatu's government, donors, and nongovernmental organizations (NGOs). Implementing these recommendations will help ensure not only a level playing field for women but also a better business environment for all entrepreneurs in Vanuatu.

Notes

1. The *National Plan of Action for Women 2007–2011* was published in 2007 with AusAID support after widespread national consultations.
2. The 2008 Human Development Index ranks Vanuatu 123rd out of 179 countries (www.hdr.undp.org/en/statistics/).
3. The World Bank's *Doing Business* index provides objective measures of business regulations and their enforcement across 181 countries (www. doingbusiness.org).
4. In his 2008 foreword to the government's budget, the Minister of Finance identified reducing the cost of doing business in Vanuatu as a key ingredient to further strong growth.
5. Interview with the acting director-general, Ministry of Justice, April 2008.

Table 2 Women in Business in Vanuatu—Promoting Women's Economic Empowerment

Recommendations for Action

Issue	Recommendation	Alignment with NPAW (relevant sections)
Vanuatu's legal framework: The system discriminates against women in some important respects, inhibiting their business success.	Clarify the relationship between custom and formal law and the apparent contradiction between the constitutional guarantee of equality and the recognition of discriminatory custom law.	
	Ensure better female representation in Parliament and on decision-making bodies, for example, by adopting a constitutional requirement for 30 percent female representation on such bodies.	
	Ensure that the recently enacted Family Protection Order Bill is implemented to give women proper protection in cases of domestic violence.	
	Amend key discriminatory laws, such as the Matrimonial Causes Act and the Citizenship Act, to end discrimination against women regarding matrimonial property and other gender-related issues.	
Unavailability of sex-disaggregated data: Lack of data, in particular on women in the private sector, makes it difficult to understand the challenges facing women and thus to design appropriate interventions.	Strengthen data collection on women in the private sector. Ensure that all future surveys on private sector activities are sex-disaggregated and the data analyzed and reported. This could include conducting separate gender analysis of the Household and Income Expenditure Survey and the Agriculture Census.	6
	Ensure that the planned Governance for Growth gender survey includes questions on women's business activities.	
	Consider using the International Monetary Fund's General Data Dissemination System, which assists in disseminating and collating sound economic, financial, and sociodemographic data.	

(continued)

13

Table 2   Women in Business in Vanuatu—Promoting Women's Economic Empowerment *(Continued)*

Issue	Recommendation	Alignment with NPAW (relevant sections)
Business start-up and licensing: Starting a business in Vanuatu is costly, time consuming, and disadvantageous to women. The fee schedule imposed on women microentrepreneurs is too expensive and may drive some of them out of business.	Streamline the Companies Act in accordance with international best practice, making company formation simpler and abolishing complex and technical legal concepts.	Modified 6.4.1
	Streamline the cooperatives regime, so that it imposes no greater regulatory burden than the reformed Companies Act. Consider distinguishing between trading and nontrading cooperatives and tailor the regulation accordingly.	
	Abolish the requirement for the registration of business names.	
	Review the business licensing regime. Consider abolition of the regime, or at least exemption for microenterprises or a reduction in fees to better reflect their income levels.	
Access to land: Women have user rights, but rarely decision-making rights over land.	Ensure that the AusAID Pacific Land program incorporates gender issues in its research, such as carrying out case studies on the effects of customary land ownership on women.	
	Require the Land Department to sex-disaggregate land titles and publicize data on the percentage of land titles held in women's names.	
	Explore compulsory joint titling and equal land rights after divorce.	
	Implement the National Land Summit recommendation for research into gender roles relating to land, and encourage chiefs to support women's participation in land matters and to promote women's traditional leadership roles.	
	Mainstream consultation with women stakeholders in government administration processes relating to land (such as granting of land leases, environmental impact assessments, and infrastructure development).	
	Provide more information about and be proactive in ensuring that women's overriding rights to land (such as rights of way and rights to use the land) are registered through the land registry.	

Issue	Action	
	Enhance the participation of women on land boards and committees.	
	Encourage the National Land Steering Committee to include in its public awareness campaign about land reform a campaign educating Vanuatu about the benefits of including women in decision making and the risks to social security when they are marginalized in land matters.	
Access to markets: Many women, particularly in the handicrafts industry, lack much needed knowledge of product development, pricing, and tailoring their products to tourist tastes.	Provide access to basic market training for women in the handicrafts industry, to help them diversify their products and improve product quality and design to better target the tourist market.	6.1.3
	Consider partnerships with tourist operators who have a vested interest in improving the quality of handicrafts.	6.1.2
Lack of awareness of "value added" and fair trade brands and certification: Networks developing fair trade markets for Pacific women and men producers are poorly resourced and lack support. Entry barriers to certification for Pacific producers and lack of certification and labeling options for fair trade handicrafts exclude women, especially from value-added market opportunities.	Provide information sessions and training to relevant regional and national bureaucracies on fair trade market opportunities and benefits.	6.3.1
	Provide financial assistance and in-country support to key fair trade organizations and networks.	
	Fund further research on fair trade in Vanuatu and the Pacific to investigate barriers to small producers' and artisans' access to the fair-trade certification system and alternative fair-trade market opportunities.	
Business and financial management skills: Lack of understanding of basic business and financial management skills and procedures limits the success of many women's businesses.	Explore feasibility for a business center or incubator that assists female entrepreneurs with small business issues and business advice.	6.3
	Provide training on very basic business skills to women microentrepreneurs, in particular VANWODS clients. Training may need to be conducted in the local language, and partnerships with commercial banks could be explored.	

(continued)

Table 2   Women in Business in Vanuatu—Promoting Women's Economic Empowerment (*Continued*)

Issue	Recommendation	Alignment with NPAW (*relevant sections*)
Access to finance: Women in Vanuatu are benefiting from microfinance schemes, but the absence of a credit reference system means that their loan repayment histories are not readily accessible and transferable. A new personal property secured transactions law has the potential to improve the collateral system for women, enabling them to use assets other than land as collateral for loans.	In the development of a regional credit bureau through the IFC's Financial Markets Infrastructure Program, support the collection of sex-disaggregated data.	6.2.1
	Support the recommendations of the UN Financial Services Sector Assessment to promote a regional program of support for expanding the reach of financial services, including innovative new partnerships, such as that between VANWODS and the National Bank of Vanuatu on the outer islands, and new products and delivery channels, such as mobile phone banking once the telecommunications infrastructure is upgraded.	
	Expedite implementation of the new Personal Property Secured Transactions Act and the establishment of a new electronic registry to support it.	
Lack of awareness among women of the benefits of bank financing for business expansion, or of the willingness of banks to lend to them based on good credit histories, may prevent women from seeking bank loans for business purposes.	Investigate with commercial banks and financial houses the potential to develop relevant new products in line with the Personal Property Secured Transactions Act and undertake outreach programs associated with the new law, especially those aimed at women.	
	Provide financial literacy training for women borrowers, as well as training on how to write a bankable business plan.	
Contract enforcement	Within the framework of IFC's alternative dispute resolution procedures, train female mediators and run a public awareness campaign on the benefits of mediation, including a component of the campaign that targets female entrepreneurs.	

Discriminatory employment law	Pass another amendment to the Employment Act to address the night-working provisions for women.	
Successful women in business are rarely visible as role models.	Encourage annual women's business awards, similar to those sponsored by Westpac Corporation in Tonga.	6.1.1
	Promote positive role models by publishing and widely disseminating research (such as this book) on women entrepreneurs.	
Women in business are not well organized.	Support the strengthening of the newly formed women's business association.	
	Support the building of knowledge and networking resources through women's business incubators.	
Women business leaders need to be developed.	Provide relevant leadership training and mentoring for women in business and decision making.	6.1.1
Women's voices need to be heard on business issues.	Establish a regional business council for women and support network development, through activities such as an annual conference.	6.3.4
	Conduct Australian Business Women's Network Advocacy Training in Vanuatu.	

Source: Authors.
Note: NPAW is the National Plan of Action for Women.

CHAPTER 1

Doing Business in Vanuatu: The Cultural, Political, Economic, and Legal Contexts for Women's Economic Empowerment

[A]lthough human rights are enshrined in the constitutions and legislation of PICTs [Pacific island countries and territories], institutional, attitudinal, and social barriers often prevent women from gaining full protection of their legal systems or exercising their legal rights. Cultural beliefs, religious practices and social bias, and a lack of awareness of legal rights hinder the exercise of rights.

— The Pacific Platform for Action

Cultural Context

Gender Equality Is a Complex Notion in Vanuatu

The concept of gender equality is by no means universally accepted in Vanuatu. Although enshrined in parts of the country's constitution, it is sometimes disregarded as donor-driven or a Western feminist ideal irrelevant to Pacific cultures. The Pacific Platform for Action, the Pacific's contribution to the Beijing Platform for Action, gives a sense of what Pacific women want for the future:

- To allow and accept desires for modern development to integrate with the relevant elements of our traditions and culture to enhance "the good life" (para 57).
- Assurance that the law upholds women's rights to equal opportunity in all fields of employment (85).
- Support for women's participation in income-generating activities in rural areas and in disadvantaged households as well as in women-headed households (85) (Secretariat of the Pacific Community 2005).

Given the multiplicity of tribal societies spread across Vanuatu's 65 islands, the issues facing women can vary considerably. The majority of tribes are patriarchal, but some are matriarchal and tribal lore differs significantly as a consequence. Across Vanuatu, however, societies place a strong emphasis on family and on women's role as nurturers—the protectors of culture and the land. For many Pacific women, their identity is associated with religious worship, *kastom* (custom), family, and motherhood.

The government's 2004 report on the UN Convention on the Elimination of All Forms of Discrimination against Women (CEDAW) (Office of the Prime Minister 2004) describes the key role played by ni-Vanuatu[1] women in the rural subsistence economy:

> [W]omen play a critical role . . . devoting most of their working lives balancing their time between meeting family as well as community needs and cultural obligations. Women's work includes an array of work from . . . caring for children, old people, people with disabilities and the infirm to domestic tasks such as fetching of water and firewood, cleaning the house, washing clothes, cooking food and gardening. Women are involved in food production including animal husbandry and production of handicrafts such as mats, baskets for the home as well as weaving of mats, baskets and grass skirts for sale as well as for cultural purposes. Nearly all women in rural areas also participate actively in church activities and participate in meetings organized within the community. . . .

Balancing such an array of economic and noneconomic tasks suggests that ni-Vanuatu women may bear a disproportionate burden of the new economic pressures. With the increasing penetration of cash into subsistence economies, there is more pressure on women to spend more time earning money, sometimes in conflict with their traditional roles and associated community status. The need to pay school fees is an important driver. According to a recent AusAID report (Cox and others 2007):

> Women are becoming more involved in income-earning activities whether by traveling to the market to sell produce or taking on more of the agricultural labor in the absence of their husbands. . . . One might expect that the entry of women into the formal economy would result in their economic empowerment, and a consequent increase in social status. However, according to the ni-Vanuatu women interviewed for this study, the opposite is generally the case. Within rural communities, the status of women depends upon how active they are in their community roles, including church and women's groups, and the contribution they make in caring for the elderly and vulnerable. When women are obliged to increase their involvement in income-earning activities, in addition to their domestic roles, they have little time left for other activities, and consequently suffer a loss of status. . . .

Yet Women's Traditional Status Is Generally Low, and They Are Marginalized in Decision Making

Traditionally, men have cultural dominance in Vanuatu society. Men achieve status through the control of knowledge (Bolton 1998, 2003), and political leadership is perceived to be a masculine role in Vanuatu. Women's leadership is less public, although there are variations in the traditional role played by women across the country (box 1.1). Church treasurers tend to be female, and women influence decision making in the home rather than in public forums.

Box 1.1

Variations in the Traditional Role of Women in Vanuatu Society

In most areas, such as the island of Tanna, communities operate on a patriarchal basis, with men being the administrators, and women's roles being highly restricted.

In a few matriarchal societies in central Vanuatu, such as Epi, women can attain the title of chief, but the role of administrator is delegated to her brother or other male relative. In other areas, such as North Ambae and North Pentecost, women traditionally play important roles in succession, inheritance, and peacemaking.

Source: Office of the Prime Minister 2004.

Gender roles in Vanuatu have been shaped by *kastom*, which refers to certain practices or beliefs that distinguish ni-Vanuatu from other people. Designating something as *kastom* has great potency in Vanuatu. The uncertain futures associated with modernity cause some ni-Vanuatu to hold tight to *kastom*. *Kastom* can be used to curtail the actions of women (Jolly 1994). Bride price, for example, while intended to celebrate the union of families, has been used to undermine women (Naviti 2003). The late Grace Mera Molisa, ni-Vanuatu poet and women's activist, asserted that women were oppressed both by traditional structures and by introduced structures of church and politics (Molisa 1991).

Despite the uncertain play of *kastom*, ni-Vanuatu women have achieved significant improvements in health and education. The Education Act of 2001 specifically legislates against discrimination based on sex for enrollment of school children, and gender parity has been achieved at the primary and secondary levels. Despite these gains, females remain underrepresented in vocational, technical, and tertiary education. Fewer females than males apply for scholarships. In 2004 only 35 percent of applications were from females (Vanuatu Rural Development and Training Centers Association 2007). Women also enjoy improved access to health care, although birth rates remain high, and teenage pregnancy and sexually transmitted diseases are on the increase (Piau-Lynch 2007).

Domestic Violence against Women Is Rife

There is strong and deeply worrying anecdotal evidence of the prevalence of domestic violence against women in Vanuatu.[2] Accurate data are hard to come by, partly because of underreporting of rape and domestic violence to the police. Yet the experience of NGOs, such as the Vanuatu Women's Center, which has an extensive network of counseling centers in all six provinces, suggests that the problem is increasing or that more cases are being reported (Office of the Prime Minister 2004). While donors have supported NGOs that work on the issue, systems for dealing with cases of rape and domestic violence remain weak, with a prevailing culture of impunity.

For example, a family protection order bill was drafted in 1997 but took more than a decade to pass through the legal system. Among other reforms, this legislation aims to introduce a statutory system of interim protection orders for victims of domestic violence. Opposition by traditional and church leaders to the perceived shift of jurisdiction from them to the formal justice system has brought the legislation under presidential scrutiny for noncompliance with the Christian principles enshrined in the constitution and some specific fundamental rights stated therein. The

Supreme Court ruled in late 2008 that the bill was to be signed by the president, which occurred in December 2008.

Meanwhile, in 2001 a new court rule (Domestic Violence Protection Order, Number 67) was introduced that enabled women to apply for interim protection orders ex parte[3] through a simple procedure. However, limited legal literacy and poor access to legal advice has meant that very few orders have been made in practice, and there is concern about poor execution of the orders by the police, despite establishment of a Family Protection Unit (Vanuatu Rural Development and Training Centers Association 2007).

Traditional justice systems also often fail to deal adequately with cases of domestic violence. For example, *kastom faen* (customary fines, which can include mats, kava, or chickens) are often the punishment imposed in cases of physical and sexual assaults (Office of the Prime Minister 2004).

Political Context

Women Are Underrepresented in Senior Leadership Positions and Politics

The cultural dominance of men is mirrored in their political leadership. Since 1980 only four women have been elected to Parliament. Female representation in provincial and municipal councils is also low. There has been only one female lord mayor in the country, in Luganville (Piau-Lynch 2007). There have been no female councilors in the six provincial councils since 1994, despite a legal requirement for these councils to include women among their elected members and appointed representatives (box 1.2) (Cox and others 2007).

Female political participation rates are an international benchmark for gender equality. With only two female members of Parliament in 2006, Vanuatu ranked among the worst in the world; 1 of 13 ministers was female (Office of the Prime Minister 2004). Women made up 21 percent of senior officials, legislators, and managers, according to a 2000 labor market survey (Vanuatu Statistics Office 2000). Vanuatu's National Plan of Action for Women has set a goal of raising women's representation in Parliament to 30 percent by 2015.

A 2002 study by the Department of Women's Affairs on why women in Vanuatu are so underrepresented politically highlighted cultural reasons (*kastom*) and the reluctance of political parties to adopt women candidates. Encouragingly, there are moves to address the issue. In November 2006 the political parties committed themselves to adopting more

Box 1.2

Restricted Leadership Roles for Women on Ambae Island, Penama Province

The Penama Provincial Council has 15 elected and 7 appointed members. The elected members are almost always men. The nominated members should include one women's and two youth representatives.

In addition to the provincial council, Ambae has an Island Council of Chiefs, the members of which are elected by the chiefs of all the villages around the island. Chiefs are always men.

Women have their own island council called *Vavine bulu*, meaning women together. Women in all the villages elect members to the council, which meets three or four times a year. Representatives from *Vavine bulu* attend the biannual conference of the National Council of Women, a nongovernmental organization.

At the village level, women's groups may be organized by churches or by the women's network, but usually each village has only one women's group, and it is that group that sends representatives to *Vavine bulu*.

Source: Tarisesei 1998.

women candidates, and the NGO Vanuatu Women in Politics is organizing women to run as independent candidates. In 2003 the Electoral Commission recommended an amendment to the Representation of the People Act to ensure that 30 percent of parliamentary seats are reserved for women, and the government has said it will adopt this amendment by 2015. At the provincial level, the Shefa Provincial Council is actively promoting increased female representation in local politics.[4]

Economic Context

Vanuatu Has Experienced Solid Economic Growth

Vanuatu has experienced strong economic growth over the last five years (estimated at nearly 6.5 percent in 2007), largely driven by foreign investment. But small-scale agriculture is still responsible for the livelihoods of 80 percent of the population, who live in "subsistence affluence," benefiting from Vanuatu's generally abundant fertile land and favorable climate (Economic Intelligence Unit 2008). Agriculture accounts for about 20 percent of the country's gross domestic product, with services accounting for a further 60 percent (figure 1.1). Nearly all exports are primary,

Figure 1.1   Sectoral Shares of GDP, 2005

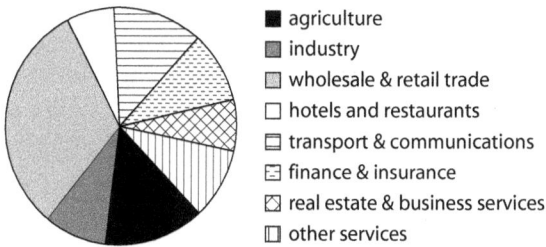

- agriculture
- industry
- wholesale & retail trade
- hotels and restaurants
- transport & communications
- finance & insurance
- real estate & business services
- other services

Source: National Accounts, Vanuatu Statistics Office.

unprocessed agricultural commodities, especially copra and cocoa, produced mainly by small-holder farmers.

Vanuatu has few large businesses; nearly 70 percent of its firms have receipts of less than $50,000 a year. Most are operated as sole proprietorships (PEDF 2003). Over 90 percent of businesses are located in the two major urban centers of Port Vila and Luganville (Vanuatu Statistics Office 2000). Most businesses tend to be focused in a few sectors—small retails outlets, buses and taxis, kava bars, and catering (Cox and others 2007).

Recent economic growth has been fueled by a land boom. Relatively cheap beachfront land has attracted significant investment from Australian and New Zealand developers. The Lands Department estimates that over 90 percent of the land on Efate, Vanuatu's main island, has now been alienated. Limited access to land rights means that women have been largely excluded from the economic benefits that this investment has brought (see chapter 3 on registering property). Vanuatu is also a center for offshore financial services, which accounts for about 10 percent of GDP (ADB 2006).

According to the World Travel and Tourism Council, tourism accounted for 35 percent of total employment in 2008. The Vanuatu Tourism Department does not keep sex-disaggregated statistics, but significant numbers of women are engaged in the tourism sector, both as employees and as entrepreneurs.

Women Are Underrepresented in the Formal Labor Force

Vanuatu has the lowest formal sector employment in the Pacific region, estimated at under 15 percent in 2004 (Luthria and others 2006). Women represent 33 percent of employees in the formal sector, where they are employed mainly as clerks, service workers, and government services workers (table 1.1). Interestingly, women in the formal sector have slightly higher average salaries than men (VT 38,800 versus VT 37,000). Only 36 women in the 2000 labor market survey were engaged as skilled agriculture and fisheries workers, compared with 460 men (although this figure does not account for women's substantial role in subsistence agriculture).

Data on Women in Private Sector Development in Vanuatu Are Limited

The Vanuatu Investment Promotion Agency, the Financial Services Commission, and the Customs and Inland Revenue Department—all gatekeepers to formalizing a business—do not disaggregate data on business entry by gender. According to the 1999 census, women owned 27 percent of all businesses, although only 2 percent of overall census respondents indicated that they were either a businessman or a businesswoman (table 1.2). According to the Chamber of Commerce and Industry of Vanuatu, couples often register businesses together, even if the wife runs the business operations. The chamber does not keep data on the gender of the business owner.

The lack of in-depth data on the business sector makes it impossible to obtain a comprehensive picture of challenges facing women in business, and there is a great need for surveys sex-disaggregated to provide such information.

Table 1.1   2000 Labor Market Survey by Type of Occupation and Sex, 2000

Occupation	Female	Male	Total	Percent female
Legislators, senior officials, managers	280	1,035	1,315	21
Professions, technicians, associated professionals	1,375	2,157	3,532	39
Clerks	1,060	693	1,753	60
Service and sales workers	1,146	1,437	2,583	44
Skilled agriculture and fishery workers	36	424	460	8
Crafts and related workers	77	1.418	1,495	5
Plant/machine operators, assemblers	52	813	865	6
Elementary occupations	658	1,611	2,269	29
Total	4,684	9,588	14,272	33

Source: Vanuatu Statistics Office 2000.

Table 1.2   Economically Active Population by Employment Status and Gender, 1999

	Female		Male		Total	
Employment status	Number	%	Number	%	Number	%
Businessman/woman	375	27	998	73	1,373	2
Government employee	1,770	37	3,074	63	4,848	6
Other employee	4,368	36	7,814	64	12,182	16
Working in the garden	26,295	49	27,442	51	53,737	70
Helping family business (no pay)	482	34	927	66	1,409	2
Voluntary community worker	108	35	203	65	311	0
Pastor/religious leader	109	15	599	85	708	1
Other position (no money)	333	68	154	32	487	1
Not stated	458	35	857	65	1,315	2
Total	34,298	45	42,072	55	76,370	100

Source: Vanuatu Statistics Office 2000.

Table 1.3   Trends in Secondary School Enrollments, 1996–2006

	1996		2001		2006	
Province	Female	Male	Female	Male	Female	Male
Malampa	367	460	555	595	839	770
Penama	540	508	668	675	826	897
Sanma	610	800	843	976	1,165	1,191
Shefa	1,051	1,167	1,660	1,659	2,622	2,358
Tafea	225	297	496	486	1,093	795
Torba	69	65	62	71	57	78
Subtotal	2,862	3,297	4,284	4,462	6,602	6,089
Total		6,159		8,746		12,691
Percent female	46		49		52	

Source: Lapi and Jimmy 2006.

The Lack of Appropriate Skills Affects Women's Economic Opportunities and Their Ability to Run Successful Businesses

Although national statistics show considerable improvement in gender parity at the secondary level (table 1.3), anecdotal evidence from interviews with banks, business development services providers, and women entrepreneurs indicates low levels of literacy and numeracy as well as limited business management and technical skills. Considerable need for these was expressed among the businesswomen interviewed for this research (appendix 1).

Legal Context

Vanuatu has an unusual legal heritage, having been administered as a joint French and British Condominium (joint territory) between 1906 and independence in 1980. The 1980 constitution provides for both English and French law to apply. However, in practice, most lawyers and judges have been trained in the English system and rely on English-based statutes and the English common law system.

In practice, the formal legal system is generally relevant only to the 30 percent of Vanuatu's population who live in the urban and peri-urban areas of Port Vila (on the island of Efate) and Luganville (on the northern island of Espiritu Santo) (Cox and others 2007). In rural areas, where 70 percent of the population lives, custom law administered primarily by chiefs, who are nearly always men, prevails. Custom law operates in parallel with the formal legal system and is enshrined in the Vanuatu Constitution (box 1.3). Other legislation such as the Criminal Procedure Act also allows for courts to take the *kastom* system into account, enabling the courts to promote reconciliation through customary processes and to take customary settlement practices into account when determining the sentence.

Box 1.3

Vanuatu's Constitution and Custom Law

The following are relevant portions of the Vanuatu Constitution on the role of customary laws in the legal system.
- "Customary laws shall continue to have effect as a part of the law of the Republic." Article 95(3)
- "If there is no rule of law applicable to a matter before it, a court shall determine the matter according to substantial justice and whenever possible in conformity with custom." Article 47(1)
- "The rules of custom shall form the basis of ownership and use of land." Article 74
- "One of the fundamental duties of every person is to bring children up with a true understanding of Vanuatu custom and cultures." Article 7
- "Village or island courts will have jurisdiction over customary matters." Article 52
- "The National Council of Chiefs (*Malvatumauri*) may be consulted in connection with any bill, particularly relating to custom and tradition." Article 30(2)

Vanuatu Has Ratified CEDAW...

Vanuatu ratified the Convention on the Elimination of All Forms of Discrimination against Women (CEDAW) without any reservations in 1995. In 2005 it ratified the Equal Remuneration Convention, and the Discrimination (Employment and Occupation) Convention, and in 2006 it ratified the Optional Protocol to the Convention.[5] But the government's 2004 CEDAW report highlighted the comment made by Chief Noel Mariasua, chairman of the *Malvatumauri* (National Council of Chiefs) on the National Day of Women in 1995, when he warned Vanuatu's women "not to take the Convention for the Elimination of All Forms of Discrimination against Women to start thinking highly of themselves and forgetting their place in society."

...and Vanuatu's Constitution Guarantees Nondiscrimination

Article 5 of the Vanuatu Constitution guarantees fundamental rights and freedoms and prohibits discrimination, including on the basis of sex. It goes further and makes provision for specific programs to advance disadvantaged groups, including women (box 1.4).

Vanuatu's penal code backs up these provisions. It makes unlawful discrimination a criminal offence.[6] However, it should be noted that there are no reported judgments of prosecutions under this provision (Jalal 1998).

But the Extent of These Guarantees and Their Relation with Custom Law Is Unclear

The precise effect of the constitution's equality provisions is unclear. They clearly bind the state, and discriminatory laws made by Parliament can be declared unconstitutional by the courts. But what is less clear is the extent to which the constitutional provisions can be applied to discriminatory acts on the part of individuals, although the penal code addresses this matter to some extent.

Another key weakness is that the provisions in the constitution that enshrine custom law seem to be in direct conflict with the constitution's equality provisions. Women often do not fare well when using custom law in resolving family law disputes. The customary law as applied by the chiefs places priority on the family's interests rather than on the individual woman's interests. But the relationship between the formal legal system and custom law is still being developed by the courts (box 1.5).

Box 1.4

Constitutional Provisions on Gender Equality

"The Republic of Vanuatu recognizes that, subject to any restrictions imposed by law on non-citizens, all persons are entitled to the following fundamental rights and freedoms of the individual without discrimination on the grounds of race, place of origin, religious or traditional beliefs, political opinions, language or sex but subject to respect for the rights and freedoms of others and to the legitimate public interest in defense, safety, public order, welfare and health-

(a) life;
(b) liberty;
(c) security of the person;
(d) protection of the law;
(e) freedom from inhuman treatment and forced labor;
(f) freedom of conscience and worship;
(g) freedom of expression;
(h) freedom of assembly and association;
(i) freedom of movement;
(j) protection for the privacy of the home and other property and from unjust deprivation of property;
(k) equal treatment under the law or administrative action, except that no law shall be inconsistent with this sub-paragraph insofar as it makes provision for the special benefit, welfare, protection or advancement of females, children and young persons, members of under-privileged groups or inhabitants of less developed areas."

The relationship between the two has been considered by the courts and has resulted in conflicting decisions. In a 1993 case, for example, the Supreme Court upheld the prosecution of a husband, who in accordance with custom law had forcibly taken his wife back to the village.[7] The court held that the constitutional guarantee of liberty of people and freedom of movement took priority over custom law. The court noted that consideration should be given to amending the constitution to clarify the role of the chiefs, adding that such an amendment was the only way that the fundamental rights of women could be protected.

The Supreme Court made a similar decision in 1995, when it held that Article 5 of the constitution granting equal rights to men and women

Box 1.5

Relationship between Formal Law and *Kastom*

Case law appears to limit the application of custom law and provides guidance
that implies custom law must comply with the Vanuatu Constitution:

Custom law should apply only if there is no legislation or relevant common
law. In a 1996 case the Supreme Court affirmed that Vanuatu law recognized the
customary practice of paying damages in cases of adultery. But it stated that custom law should apply only if there was no legislation or relevant common law
and the custom is not unjust or against the constitution (*Banga v. Waiwo,* VUSC 5).

Custom claims can be made only when customary arrangements apply. In a
1998 case, the Supreme Court held that there could be no custom claim in relation to a marriage that had not been entered into as a customary marriage (*Molu
v. Molu* No 2, VUSC 15).

overrides Article 72, which says "the rules of custom shall form the basis
of ownership and use of land."[8] The court said that Article 5 is a fundamental principle that overrides any law or custom contrary to it. The
court went on to say that a decision giving more rights to women than to
men would be contrary to CEDAW, taking the view that although the
convention was not directly part of domestic law, the government, by rat-
ifying CEDAW, had created a legitimate expectation that it would act in
accordance with the convention's principles.

In 2003 the Court of Appeal noted that Article 5 of the constitution
guaranteeing equal treatment for women under the law may apply to the
case of the division of matrimonial property.[9] However, the court said
these constitutional principles were aspirational (rather than fundamental as discussed in the 1995 case) and had to be translated by Parliament
into law. The court stated that Parliament had to decide how Vanuatu
could reflect CEDAW in its domestic law, taking into account the
changes it wanted to see in the social patterns of men and women and
how these changes should occur.

Laws that Discriminate against Women Remain
on the Statute Book

Despite the ratification of CEDAW, Vanuatu's statute book still contains
laws that directly discriminate against women and require amendment to
remove discriminatory provisions. Women's NGOs have advocated for

amendments to the constitution to better enshrine nondiscrimination principles. A study commissioned by Vanuatu Women in Politics in the late 1990s found that out of 208 laws reviewed, 12 discriminated against women, including in the areas of marriage, sexual offenses, labor and employment, and rent (Office of the Prime Minister 2004). Some of these laws relate directly to women's ability to participate in the economy, and others affect the status of women more generally. Unlike those of Fiji and Tuvalu, Vanuatu's constitution does not contain a provision enabling the courts directly to apply international conventions, and the extent to which CEDAW can be directly applied in Vanuatu is being worked out through the courts.

Recommendations

- Encourage strategic litigation to clarify scope of Article 5 of the constitution on antidiscrimination and the direct application of CEDAW in relation to property rights.
- Amend domestic statutes to bring them into line with CEDAW.
- Consider how the constitution can be amended to prioritize rights over custom where there is a conflict.
- Increase dialogue with the *Malvatumauri* to enable them to make and accept decisions that are consistent with the rights granted by the constitution.

Notes

1. *Ni-Vanuatu* refers to all Melanesian ethnicities originating in Vanuatu.
2. AusAID's Office of Development Effectiveness has produced a report "Violence against Women in Melanesia and East Timor: Building on Global and Regional Promising Approaches," which makes recommendations for future support to reduce violence against women.
3. An ex parte decision is one made by a judge without requiring all the parties to the controversy to be present.
4. In May 2004 Shefa Provincial Council adopted CEDAW as its platform for action for women in the province, with the express aim of achieving 30 percent female representation in decision-making positions. The provincial government has widely disseminated information on CEDAW. (Office of the Prime Minister 2004).
5. The protocol contains a communications procedure that allows individuals to submit complaints to the CEDAW Committee.

6. Section 150 provides that "no person shall discriminate against another person with respect to his right to the supply of any goods or services, or to gain or to continue in any employment, or to be admitted to any public place, by reason of the sex, ethnic or racial origin . . . of any such person."

7. *Public Prosecutor v. Kota*, Criminal Case 58 (1993), [1989–1994] 2 Van LR 661.

8. *John Noel v. Obed Toto* (1995), Supreme Court of Vanuatu 18 (1994), Luganville.

9. *Joli v. Joli* (2003), Civil Appeal 11 (2003), Port Vila.

CHAPTER 2

Starting and Licensing a Business

There are 1,300 locally-owned companies formally registered in Vanuatu, and another 5,000 registered as overseas companies.

Foreign Investment Advisory Services 2007

Starting a Business in Vanuatu Is Costly and Time Consuming by International Standards

Vanuatu ranks 94th out of 181 countries on the ease of starting a business (figure 2.1). The process costs nearly 55 percent of the country's annual per capita income and takes 39 days (table 2.1). That compares with a cost of 0.4 percent of per capita income and a time of one day in New Zealand, the top ranking country in *Doing Business in 2009* (World Bank 2008).

There are a number of legal routes to setting up a business in Vanuatu. The appropriate route depends on the status of the investor and on the desired status of the business (table 2.2). The World Bank's Doing Business indicators focus on the costs of a local investor registering a limited liability company. In fact, less than 30 percent of businesses in Vanuatu operate on this basis (PEDF 2003). The vast majority are operating as sole traders or as partnerships. But companies are frequently regarded as the optimum business form. They give the owners

Figure 2.1   Starting a Business—Rankings for Vanuatu and Comparator Economies

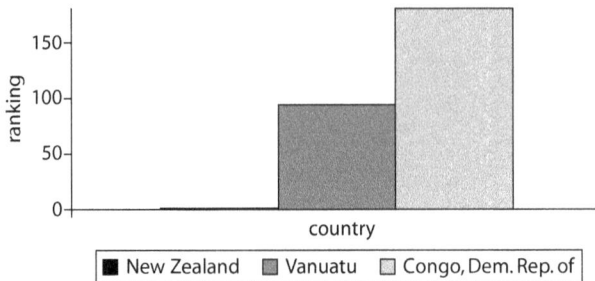

Source: World Bank 2008.

Table 2.1   Starting a Business—Benchmarking in the *Doing Business* Index

Indicator	Vanuatu	Region	OECD
Procedures (number)	8	8.6	5.8
Duration (days)	39	44.2	13.4
Cost (% GNI per capita)	54.8	32.3	4.9
Paid in minimum share capital (% GNI per capita)	0	37.3	19.7

Source: World Bank 2008.

the protection of limited liability status, encouraging risk taking and entrepreneurship. The division of ownership of the company into shares facilitates changes in ownership, enabling businesses to continue beyond the life of the original owners, as well as facilitating investment by third parties. The legal structure they provide facilitates the survival and growth of the business.

Company formation in Vanuatu is based on the regime that existed in the United Kingdom in 1948. It requires the preparation and filing of a number of documents, which realistically are likely to require the assistance of either a lawyer or a company formation agent (box 2.1). The legislation allows the relevant minister to refuse an application for registration. The government of Vanuatu has recognized that more businesses would likely incorporate if company formation were easier, quicker, and certain. A fundamental review of Vanuatu's Companies Act is therefore taking place, with a view to producing a white paper setting out options for reform, followed by new legislation.

It is anticipated that Vanuatu's company law will be streamlined in line with international best practice, currently to be found in New Zealand

Table 2.2   Routes to Starting a Business in Vanuatu

Status of investor(s)	Status of business	Legislative framework for business entry
Overseas investor(s)	Offshore company (for tax reasons)	*International Companies Act of 1992* exempts companies for 20 years from tax on profits, capital gains, or distributions, stamp duty, and exchange control restrictions. Not allowed to carry on business with or raise money from the public in Vanuatu. Otherwise same requirements for setting up a company as a local investor.
Overseas investor(s)	Local company	*Companies Act of 1986* has same requirements for setting up a company as a local investor. *Foreign Investment Act of 1998* provides for special licensing for foreign investors in local companies; the licensing regime is administered by the Vanuatu Investment Promotion Authority (VIPA). Approval for setting up a business takes about three weeks and the annual license fee ranges from VT 15,000 ($160) to VT 50,000 ($540), depending on the size of the investment. VIPA estimates that about 25 percent of the license applications are from women. *Business License Act of 1998* requires all businesses operating in Vanuatu to have a business license issued by the Department of Customs and Inland Revenue. In addition, a foreign investor must obtain a work permit (administered by the Department of Labor) and a residency permit (administered by the Department of Immigration).
Local investor(s)	Business with legal identity separate from its owner(s) and with limited liability status[a]	*Companies Act of 1986* requires incorporation of the company by registration with the Financial Services Commission in the Ministry of Finance. *Business License Act of 1998* (see above).
Local investor(s)	Business with legal identity separate from its owner(s) and with limited liability status[a] and operated under democratic, cooperative principles	*Cooperative Societies Act of 1987* requires registration of a cooperative with the Ministry for Commerce and Cooperatives. *Business License Act of 1998* (see above).

(continued)

Table 2.2   Routes to Starting a Business in Vanuatu *(Continued)*

Status of investor(s)	Status of business	Legislative framework for business entry
Local investor(s)	Business operated either as a sole trader or in partnership, without separate legal identity.	Where there is more than one owner, the *Partnership Act of 1975* provides a framework for relations between the owners. If the business is operating under a name that is not the name of the owner or one of the owners, registration with the Financial Services Commission under the *Business Names Act of 1990* is required. *Business License Act of* 1998 (see above).

Source: Authors.

a. The liability of the owner(s) is limited to the amount of the paid-in share capital of the company.

Box 2.1

Company Formation Process in Vanuatu

- Search register of company names
- Reserve desired company name
- If foreign applicant, obtain license from VIPA
- File:
  — Memorandum
  — Articles of association
  — Information regarding directors and secretary
  — Statement of nominal capital
  — Notice of registered office
  — Declaration of compliance
- Pay fee (ranging from VT 30,000 ($325) to VT 250,000 ($2,700)

---

and Australia. Key reforms would simplify company formation processes so that one simple application form is required; abolish the complex company law concepts of nominal capital, par value shares, and *ultra vires* that complicate both company formation and ongoing company administration;[1] and allow sole-person companies rather than requiring two members as is currently the case. This last point would enable even microenterprises, where women's businesses are more likely to be found, to incorporate.

The Vanuatu Financial Services Commission, which is responsible for registering business names, does not keep sex-disaggregated data to establish how many of the 1,300 companies have been registered by women, but officials indicate that there are "many more" registrations by men than by women. There is no evidence of any form of direct discrimination against women who seek to register their businesses as companies. However, complex company formation provisions, requiring the assistance of a professional, are likely to be a particular problem for women, who may be less business savvy than their male counterparts. Reforms to simplify and streamline Vanuatu's Companies Act could therefore be of particular benefit to women entrepreneurs.

Cooperatives: An Alternative Business Form

Ten percent of businesses in Vanuatu are registered as cooperatives, and their combined membership is 20,000, an estimated 30–40 percent of which are women (PEDF 2003; Department of Cooperatives and Ni-Vanuatu Business Development Services). Like companies, cooperatives offer a convenient form for a group of individuals to form a business, benefit from limited liability status, and share profits between them.

With their values of self-help, democracy, equality, equity, and solidarity, cooperatives often combine business and a social agenda. They operate on the basis of one vote per member, and unlike companies that are based on majority control, cooperatives are designed to facilitate equal participation of all members. Cooperatives are used both for conducting businesses and for facilitating savings and loans. In Port Vila business cooperatives are involved in the retail sector, while in the provinces they are involved in fishing and agricultural (copra, kava, and cocoa) activities, according to the Department of Cooperatives and Ni-Vanuatu Business Development Services.

Vanuatu's regulatory regime for cooperatives is contained in the Cooperative Societies Act of 1987. By international standards, the regime set out in the act is cumbersome, with an unnecessarily high degree of supervision from the state (the Department of Cooperatives) (box 2.2).

Cooperatives tend to be grassroots, community-based organizations, and so the requirements for forming and running a cooperative should aim at making them as accessible a business form as possible. Regulatory controls should be kept to a minimum, consistent with adequate regulation to protect the interests of their members. At the very least, the regime for regulating cooperatives should be as straightforward as the regime for regulating companies. It should also distinguish between trading and nontrading cooperatives and should allow greater flexibility

Box 2.2

Key Elements of Regulation of Cooperatives in Vanuatu

- A minimum of seven members is required for the registration of a cooperative.
- The following information must be filed before a cooperative can be registered:
  — The name and address of the cooperative
  — Terms of admission of members
  — Mode of holding meetings
  — How the profits are applied and funds invested.
- Cooperatives have to submit annual returns and are subject to annual audits.
- Legislation places numerous restrictions on cooperatives, including:
  — Restrictions on borrowing from or lending to nonmembers
  — Restrictions on use of profits, including putting one-fourth of the profits into a statutory reserve fund annually.
  Other powers of the registrar or minister include:
  — Dissolution of the cooperative's governing committee by the registrar
  — Appointment of a special member to the committee by the minister if it is in the interest of the national economy.

for fundraising from nonmembers. Further educational programs that inform members of their rights and responsibilities within such a structure would be especially helpful in facilitating sound governance practices. Therefore, once proposals for streamlining Vanuatu's Companies Act have been developed, the Cooperative Societies Act should be reviewed and consideration given to providing a "lighter-touch" regime for cooperative regulation, aimed at reducing the time and cost of forming and running cooperatives. As with simplification of the Companies Act, it is likely that women will benefit disproportionately from such reforms.

The Business Names Registration Regime

Businesses that are not companies or cooperatives operate as sole proprietorships (if one owner) or partnerships (if more than one owner). This applies to the vast majority of both male- and female-run businesses in Vanuatu. All businesses that operate under a name that is not the surname of the owner or the surnames of the partners are required to register the business name under the Business Names Act of 1990.

Registration under this law does not confer separate legal status on a business. Rather, the purpose of registration is to "protect" business names; to allow the public to search the register to determine the names of individuals trading under a business name; and to restrict the use of certain business names, particularly those that may be misleading.

The concept of business names registration originated in England and Wales, but the regime has been recognized there as overly burdensome and has been scrapped in favor of a streamlined regime requiring permission for use only of certain potentially misleading names.

The Vanuatu Financial Services Commission, which oversees the business names registry, has no capacity to enforce the law. So in practice many small businesses are operating in Vanuatu under an unregistered business name. This fact in itself suggests that the law serves little or no purpose and should be repealed. Banks, however, may require a business name certificate as a prerequisite to lending to a small business and, to the extent this occurs, the law is imposing an unnecessary regulatory burden on businesses.

The Business Licensing Regime

All businesses operating in Vanuatu, whether owned by an expatriate or a ni-Vanuatu, require a business license from the Department of Customs and Inland Revenue. Annual renewal is required. The institutional home of this license highlights the fact that the license is in fact a tax. It serves no regulatory purpose.

The minimum business license fee of VT 5,000 ($55) applies to businesses with an annual turnover of less than VT 10 million ($100,000). But nearly 70 percent of businesses in Vanuatu have receipts of less than $50,000 a year (PEDF 2003), and many operators of microbusinesses have turnovers much less than this. Women operating microenterprises supported by VANWODS, a microfinance institution with exclusively female clients, argues that this licensing fee is prohibitively expensive for them and should be reduced (box 2.3).

Outside Port Vila and Luganville, the business license regime is operated by the six provincial governments of Malampa, Penama, Sanma, Shefa, Tafea, and Torba, each of which is empowered to collect the license fee on an annual basis from all businesses operating within its geographic boundaries. Provincial governments set their own fees, which they retain. Again, the license is in effect a tax. VANWODS has reported that some women operating small businesses have complained that the license fees are high and appear arbitrary, and they do not always receive receipts for their payments. The varying rates (table 2.3) would appear to make confusion about the level of fee more likely. Additionally, kava bar owners on Santos island are required to obtain two licenses to operate.

Business licenses account for only 2.5 percent of government's annual tax revenue. But the tax is payable by all businesses, no matter how small, and small businesses are charged a disproportionately high rate by the central government. At the local level, varying rates of license lead to a confusing regime. Women entrepreneurs often hire agents to procure

Box 2.3

Adverse Effects of Licensing on Women

VANWODS had an agreement with the Customs and Inland Revenue Department that business licenses would be issued to each VANWODS center (each center has up to 35 members), rather than issuing individual licenses to the women members. However, in 2007 the government advised that from then on each VANWODS member would have to purchase a business license. Members of VANWODS argue that the new regime is prohibitively expensive and will force many of them out of business.

Table 2.3   Shefa Business License Fees

Type of business	Vatu
Retail store	5,000
Home manufactures	2,500
Tourism	6,000
Rental house	5,000
Cooking	2,500
Sale of kerosene	2,500
Bakeries bread	2,500
Sale of fuel	2,500
Kato	5,000
Sale of drass and calico printing	2,500
Kava bar	5,000
Brick manufacture	6,500
Lawn mower	3,000
Ice cream	2,500
Other	3,000

Source: Authors.

their business licenses, paying up to VT 25,000 for a license that costs VT 5,000.

Officers of the Department of Customs and Inland Revenue, responsible for enforcing the business license laws, are constrained by resources and regard compliance as voluntary. However, they do undertake random checks. Not having a license or obstructing the search for the license can result in high penalties and imprisonment for three months. Women who are involved in the sale of food and clothing at markets have complained that they are an easy target and subject to such ad hoc checks.

Recommendations

- Streamline the Companies Act in accordance with international best practice, making company formation simpler and abolishing complex and technical legal concepts.
- Streamline the cooperatives regime, so that it imposes no greater regulatory burden than the reformed Companies Act. Consider distinguishing between trading and nontrading cooperatives and tailor the regulation accordingly.
- Abolish the requirement for the registration of business names.
- Review the business licensing regime. Consider abolition, or at least exemption, for microenterprises or a reduction in fees for microentrepreneurs to better reflect their income levels.
- Collect sex-disaggregated data at company registry and for licenses to increase understanding of female entrepreneur activity.

Note

1. The concept of nominal capital measures a company's worth by the amount of capital originally paid into it or agreed to be paid in. The par value of a share is linked to its nominal capital but is generally regarded as a misleading and confusing concept, having no relation to the true value of the share. *Ultra vires* is the concept that a company can only do what it is authorized to do by its constitution. Other acts are outside its powers and therefore void or voidable.

CHAPTER 3

Registering Property

Land is highly valued in Vanuatu, not only for what it produces, but also for what it symbolizes in terms of status and identity.

Office of the Prime Minister 2004

Land registration in Vanuatu is time consuming and costly. Vanuatu scores badly in the *Doing Business* index on registering property (table 3.1), ranking at a low 115 out of 181 economies (figure 3.1). The key issue is the length of time it takes to register—an average of 188 days, compared with 2 days in top-ranking New Zealand. The land registry in Vanuatu is not computerized, the records are disorganized, and there are some concerns about the integrity of the register with complaints of multiple registrations of the same plot of land.

The problems in the land registry are important because land is one of Vanuatu's key assets. It is generally rich, fertile, and abundant, although there is some pressure from a population that is growing at the rate of 2.4 percent a year, coupled with poor quality soil or poor water supply.[1] Land is highly valued in Vanuatu not only for what it produces but also for what it symbolizes in terms of status and identity (Office of the Prime Minister 2004).

Table 3.1   **Registering Property—Comparative Rankings**

Indicator	Vanuatu	Region	OECD
Procedures (number)	2	5	4.7
Duration (days)	188	99	30.3
Cost (% of property value)	11	4.1	4.5

Source: World Bank 2008.

Figure 3.1   **Registering Property—Vanuatu and Comparative Economies**

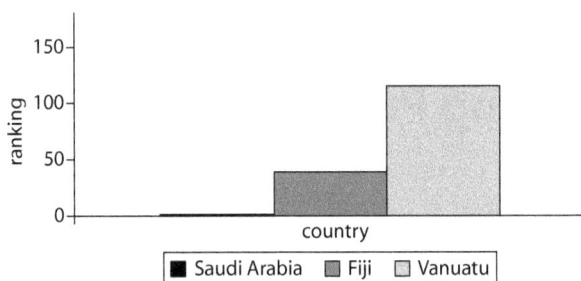

Source: World Bank 2008.

Tourism, agriculture, and the recent land boom are dependant on the ability to use land as an economic resource. On Efate, the main island in Vanuatu, about 90 percent of customary land has now been leased out, and Santo, Malekula, and Epi islands are now beginning to be developed (Economist Intelligence Unit 2007). Recently the sales have been driven by foreign investment in holiday and retirement homes.

Land Tenure in Vanuatu

Despite the recent land boom, the vast majority of land in Vanuatu is still held under customary tenure. This means that it is held according to the landholding system of the people of the area in which it is situated. Vanuatu's constitution entrenches customary landholding, providing that "all land in the Republic of Vanuatu belongs to the indigenous custom owners and their descendents." The constitution also provides for the National Council of Chiefs to be consulted on all land matters.

The basic legal framework for landholding in Vanuatu is set out in three key pieces of legislation (box 3.1). Originally intended as an interim arrangement, this system has remained in place since independence in 1980. The system is fraught with uncertainties (for example, around rights

Box 3.1

Basic Legal Framework Governing Land Ownership in Vanuatu

- The Land Reform Act of 1980 provided for all state land to be vested in the government of Vanuatu and for it to be used by its custom owners.
- The Alienated Land Act of 1982 provided for replacing freeholds and other titles in alienated land with long-term leases.
- The Land Leases Act of 1983 provided for registration of leasehold titles. It defined the procedure for lease agreements and established the lands records office.

Source: Naupa and Simo 2007.

to renew leases) and problems (for example, there is no provision for registration of customary land—only leases may be registered).

Land in Vanuatu cannot (in theory at least) be permanently alienated. Freehold does not exist. But there are instead long leases. Up to 75 years can be granted by the owner(s) of customary land for a single up-front payment, with a minimal annual ground rent. These long leases are considered almost as good as freehold. Leasehold title can be sold with the permission of the original owner or his heirs.

With high land values, high up-front payments, and strong demand for new leases, determining the ownership of customary land—and who has the power to grant a lease over the land—has become vital. Vanuatu has a wide range of customary landholding practices. These are mainly unwritten, complicated rules of inheritance and traditional practices (Jalal 1998). They range from family and clan-based holdings to individual holdings centered around the head of a nuclear family.

Women and Land Ownership

Land legislation does not directly discriminate against women. But customary landholding practices do. Commentators agree that all customary landholding systems in Vanuatu are characterized to a greater or lesser extent by the marginalization of women. Vanuatu has both *patrilineal* and *matrilineal* landholding systems. The patrilineal system is the most common, with land control and management passed through the male line. In most cases the system is also patriarchal, meaning that women do not have the right to have land passed to them. Even in matrilineal societies where land passes through the female line, women do not necessarily control or manage the land.

In practice, women in Vanuatu have very limited rights to control and manage customary land. They are marginalized from decisions about how it is used, whether it can be mortgaged to obtain loans for development, and whether it can be leased to individuals. But under custom law, women nearly always have some rights over land, in the form of *usufruct* rights—rights of use, but not of control or management (box 3.2).

Women's Rights over Customary Land Are Increasingly Threatened

Any rights a woman has over land are extinguished on registration of a lease. Usufruct rights are not noted on the register, even though the Land Leases Act provides that overriding interests, including easements and rights of way, can be registered. Furthermore, it has been argued that the imposition of external religions and gender ideologies into customary societies, and in some cases the moves to codify custom law, have increasingly excluded women from rights over land (Naupa and Simo 2007).

Box 3.2

Women's Rights over Land under Custom Law

- Women do usually have *usufruct* rights, or rights of use, while primary land rights are held by men. These usage rights typically allow a woman to use her parents' land until she marries. A married woman has usufruct rights in her husband's village. But if her husband dies, these rights are usually lost.
- Women sometimes assume a custodial right over land when no male heirs exist to inherit primary rights. In the central islands, for example, it is reported that one woman brought with her into marriage a right to specific parcels of land that she and her husband could use during her lifetime.
- In matrilineal societies, women are regarded as the source, rather than the exercisers, of land rights. Women may have rights in their mother's land before and after marriage, but their maternal uncles or their brothers usually control and manage those rights.

Source: Office of the Prime Minister 2004.

For example, according to Naupa and Simo, Raga, on the island of North Pentecost, operates a matrilineal system, with tribes consisting of matrilineal descent groups that are tied to particular areas of land. Traditionally, women may be consulted in land matters, with avenues for women to gain rank within society, permitting them access to and participation in decision-making processes. The final decision about land matters rests with the males. Gradually, however, attitudes have shifted and decisions about land are increasingly perceived as a male-only domain.

In Mele, South Efate, villagers can claim land rights through either parent, although typically the males make all land decisions and women are not active participants in the process. Customary law on Efate was codified in the Efate Vaturisu Customary Land Law of 2007. This codification has further marginalized women, with male heads of households recognized as holding the primary land rights. No women were involved in the codification discussions at the Council of Chiefs.

In another example, ni-Vanuatu women on the island of Tanna were finding expansion of their successful tourism businesses blocked by customary land tenure rules. The growing tourism industry on the island has led to the creation of several female-owned enterprises, including bungalows, guesthouses, and restaurants as well as tourist markets for crafts, clothing and food. However, interviews during a field visit to Tanna in April 2008 suggested that many of these women could not meet the growing demand for their services because they could not get access to land. Some women said they could not expand their guesthouse operations because they could not get permission from customary landowners to build more guesthouses on nearby land. According to the businesswomen, several of the landowners on Tanna initially agreed to hand over land for private development, but once the business started to grow and make profit, the customary landowners wanted to claim the land back for themselves to share in the profits. Other women noted that their business start-ups or growth were being constrained by the lack of large and low-interest business loans. An unreliable supply of power and water was also a perennial concern for those catering to tourists.

Women Are Largely Excluded from Making Decisions about Customary Land

Disputes involving custom land are in the first instance referred to the *nakamal*, an unofficial village court, where customary land principles are applied. Women are highly unlikely to be part of this process. Nor are they likely to participate if a dispute enters the formal legal system.

The Customary Land Tribunals Act of 2001 gave jurisdiction over customary land disputes to a hierarchy of customary land tribunals, starting with the village land tribunal and ending with the island land tribunal. Tribunal membership comprises chiefs and elders. These are almost always men, although there is scope to include women as elders.

Women Hold Less Than 0.1 Percent of Registered Leases

It is virtually unknown for a woman to be recognized as the owner of customary land and for a lease to be granted in her favor. Not surprisingly, therefore, only a tiny minority of registered leases are in women's names. The only way a woman can acquire title to land is to buy an existing lease in an urban area. The land registry reports that of the 30,000 registered leases, fewer than 20 are held solely by a woman (although more leases are registered in the names of both husband and wife).

The Need to Enhance Women's Rights over Land Has Been Recognized

The 2006 Vanuatu National Women's Forum and the National Land Summit placed women's access to land on the national agenda. Both were highly participatory processes. The land summit, organized by the Ministry of Lands and the Vanuatu Cultural Center, followed a series of six provincial land summits. The most pressing issues as far as women were concerned were the need for women to have a greater role in decision making about land, to be encouraged to participate in the interpretation of custom and in the granting of leases, as well as the need to ensure an adequate definition of custom owner in the legislation. The current legislation recognizes neither group ownership of custom land nor women's rights over the land. It was recognized that the current legislative framework for land administration, originally intended as an interim measure, is unsatisfactory and needs to be replaced by a coherent national land policy supported by a national land law as provided for in Vanuatu's constitution (Lunnay and others 2007). A National Land Steering Committee was subsequently formed to take forward the recommendations of the National Land Summit, and reform efforts are being supported by the Australian and New Zealand agencies for international development.

Recommendations

- Implement the National Land Summit recommendation for research into gender roles relating to land and encourage chiefs to support women's participation in land matters and to promote women's traditional leadership roles.[2]

- Mainstream consultation with women stakeholders in government administration processes relating to land (such as grants of land leases, environmental impact assessments, and infrastructure development).
- Provide more information about and be proactive in ensuring that women's overriding rights to land (such as rights of way and rights to use the land) are registered through the land registry.
- Enhance the representation of women on land boards and land committees.
- Explore compulsory joint titling and equal land rights after divorce.
- Encourage the National Land Steering Committee to include in its public awareness campaign about land reform a campaign educating Vanuatu about the benefits of including women in decision making and the risks to social security when they are marginalized from land matters.
- Expedite the computerized land registry recording system.

Notes

1. For example, Tanna, Tongoa, the Shepherds, Paama, and parts of Ambae (Cox and others 2007).
2. These recommendations were taken mainly from Naupa and Simo (2007).

CHAPTER 4

Getting Credit

Geographic isolation, demographic dispersion, limited income-generating opportunities, financial illiteracy, and traditional socio-economic structures create formidable challenges to any service provider in the Least Developed Countries (LDCs), financial services in particular.

UNDP Financial Services Sector Assessment 2007

Access to Credit Has Been a Key Constraint for Businesses in Vanuatu

The financial sector in Vanuatu is relatively large for a country at its level of development (accounting for about 7 percent of GDP and with the largest offshore financial center in the region).[1] Collectively, commercial bank deposits and loans to the private sector are 96 percent and 46 percent of GDP, respectively (UNDP 2007). These numbers are, however, distorted by large borrowers and depositors in a small population, as well as significant expatriate involvement in business. Access to financial services by the general population is low; the governor of the Reserve Bank estimates that only 10 percent of the population was formally banked in 2008.[2] The government's Priorities and Action Agenda (2006–2015) identifies the underdeveloped financial system, especially in the rural areas, as one of the major structural weaknesses in efforts to improve economic infrastructure and support services.

By international standards, businesses still find it relatively difficult to obtain formal credit, although recent reforms are expected to bring improvements. Vanuatu has recently undertaken significant reforms making it easier for businesses to use movable property as collateral and passing a new secured transactions law, the Personal Property Securities Act. As a result, its *Doing Business* ranking on obtaining credit has improved by 42 points since the previous year. While Vanuatu ranked 126 out of 179 economies on the World Bank Group's *Doing Business 2008* indicator for getting credit, it jumped to 84th out of 181 economies in the 2009 ranking (figure 4.1).

These recent reforms have set the scene for improved access to credit for businesspeople over time. This is significant because access to finance has been the most common business problem cited by entrepreneurs. Data on small and medium enterprises indicate that the most significant business constraint facing entrepreneurs in Vanuatu is the lack of working capital; 76 percent of businesses agree with the statement that it is hard to get a loan. Only 32 percent of respondents state that their businesses had received loans, and 20 percent of those consider that their loans were insufficient (PEDF 2003).

Women are particularly affected by the constraints on credit. The United Nations Development Programme's financial services assessment for Vanuatu (UNDP 2007) noted that very little information was available on the gender dimensions of access to finance in Vanuatu and across the region. The report surmised that it is reasonable to expect that women have less access to credit than men, given the discriminatory practices and laws affecting women's ownership of assets and the lower numbers of women in paid employment. Focus groups undertaken in

Figure 4.1   Getting Credit—Vanuatu and Comparator Economies

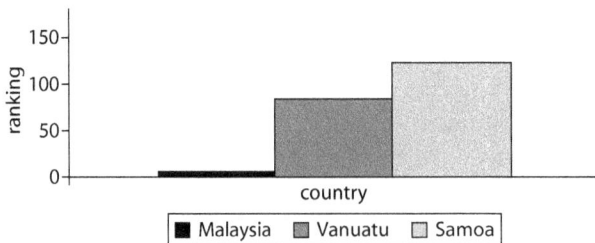

Source: World Bank 2008.

2008 with women entrepreneurs on the islands of Efate, Tanna, and Santo substantiated this assessment, with general dissatisfaction expressed relating to collateral requirements, high interest rates, and perceived sexist attitudes of bankers, especially in the outer islands. Some women complained they had to provide a guarantee from their husbands, although men were not required to get guarantees from their wives.

Women Have Some Access to Microfinance

The Vanuatu Women in Development Scheme (VANWODS), the National Bank of Vanuatu (NBV), and organizations like cooperatives and credit unions are providing financing to microbusinesses in Vanuatu without requiring collateral. Often the majority of beneficiaries are women. Of these organizations, VANWODS has probably had the most success in helping women obtain credit and is recognized as Vanuatu's only sustainable microfinance institution (UNDP 2007). Organizational provision of microfinance is important in Vanuatu, where loan sharks reportedly charge effective interest rates of close to 400 percent per year.

VANWODS began delivering microfinance services to women in 1996, and by 2007 had served more than 2,600 active members with VT 29 million in outstanding loans (box 4.1). Although not technically permitted under Vanuatu's legislative regime, VANWODS holds member savings and pays around 4 percent interest. Average member saving is VT 44,626. Most members take out two loans per year, with an average size of VT 43,087. Sixty percent of loans are used for income generation by operating, for example, retail stores, sewing businesses, and kava bars. Effective lending rates are close to 90 percent per year and the repayment rate is 98 percent. But the microfinancing nature of VANWODS operations means that women are restricted to borrowing small amounts at high interest rates, with short loan repayment periods.

Apart from VANWODS, the National Bank of Vanuatu (NBV) is operating a mobile banker operation to deliver a microfinance scheme on a number of the outer islands, involving 130 staff, many of whom tour rural areas on motorbikes. About 43 percent of loans disbursed go into small trade, mainly village shops, and about 30 percent go into agriculture, livestock, and fisheries. Operations have expanded quickly and as of April 2008 NBV had approved 1,600 loans, ranging from VT 25,000 to VT 50,000. Individual loans are provided in the $2,000 range for existing businesses only. The model used is character-based lending, with chiefs recommending who should receive finance. Chiefs are then asked to

Box 4.1

Microfinance and Small-scale Lending in Vanuatu: VANWODS

Before joining VANWODS we had no money and there was less respect. The eyes of our husbands were closed. Now that we have joined VANWODS their eyes are open wide and they pay a lot of respect.

VANWODS member

VANWODS was started as a project within the government of Vanuatu's Department of Culture, Religion, Women's Affairs and Archives. The project was initiated in response to the Vanuatu National Plan of Action for Women to provide disadvantaged women with access to microfinance and income-earning opportunities. The Grameen Bank–style solidarity lending model was adapted to local conditions, based on group guarantees and mutual trust. In 2001 VANWODS was transformed into an independent beneficiary-owned organization registered under the Charitable Associations Act of Vanuatu. The operating costs for a small stand-alone operation like VANWODS, which administers a large number of very small loans, is high, and until 2007 it was heavily subsidized. The organizational mission is to be the respected leader in the provision of financial and business development services for people to live in dignity and security by providing appropriate business development services.

This mission has met with some success, and has been instrumental in increasing the number of women's businesses in Vanuatu. According to the 2007 VANWODS Microfinance Impact Assessment:

- Ninety-seven percent of members have a business today. Before joining VANWODS, only 28 percent of these women had a business.
- The typical member increased her number of businesses by one over the past five years (compared with no change for nonmembers).
- Long-term members (five years or more) earn average profits of VT 22,700, compared to VT 14,170 five years earlier.

The most common responses to whether participation in VANWODS had led to any changes in their business:

- "Before no business no vatu. Now we join VANWODS we have income."
- "Loans have helped us to start or improve our business, which helps to generate income."
- "VANWODS makes it possible for women to make business and be self-employed."

(continued)

Box 4.1 *(Continued)*

Members commonly cited establishing and managing their own small business as the major impact of belonging to VANWODS, generating income, confidence, and respect, as well as making it possible to pay for children's education.

Top needs cited by members:

- Business skills and access to new market opportunities
- Literacy, numeracy, and financial awareness training
- Better understanding of financial products and services

Sources: Nichols 2007; interview with John Salong, managing director, VANWOODS, April 21, 2008; VANWODS Microfinance customer brochure.

intervene in cases of repayment failure. Repayment rates have been high, with 60-day arrears at 1.5 percent.

Only 15 percent of NBV loans currently go to women, but NBV management is very open to advice on how to increase this percentage and is currently in discussions with VANWODS about how best to target and serve the women's market. Encouragingly, VANWODS and NBV have also been deliberating on how best to collaborate to bridge the gap between micro- and commercial financing.[3] This kind of partnership could reduce back-office costs for VANWODS and help extend client reach for NBV. NBV is planning to further extend banking services to rural areas through electronic banking using mobile phone technology, but this will depend on telecommunications infrastructure.

Savings and loans cooperatives are primarily owned by women, who run 90 percent of the more than 30 cooperatives in Vanuatu. The cooperatives hold accounts with the NBV, and members are permitted to draw down against savings.

Women are also well represented in credit unions. The Vanuatu Credit Union League is the umbrella organization for credit unions. There are 2 credit unions with 13 savings clubs located throughout rural Vanuatu. In 2003 the league had 700 members, of whom 51 percent were women.

The National Provident Fund, which is the only compulsory savings scheme for both employers and employees, lends members back their own funds at a relatively high 12 percent for purchases such as school fees and home improvement. Business loans are being planned.[4]

Sources of Commercial Finance

Commercial finance is offered by the National Bank of Vanuatu (NBV, government owned but commercially operated); ANZ and Westpac (both Australian commercial bank subsidiaries); and BRED bank (French), which opened in April 2008. Of these, only NBV has a reasonable branch network presence outside the main centers, with 24 branches and a presence on 13 islands. An ANZ mobile banking unit now travels around the island of Efate, expanding reach for populations not close to bank branches. Financial services providers note the challenges of providing sustainable services given the geographic isolation and small and dispersed populations. Only NBV is required to cross-subsidize branch operations to extend coverage to rural areas and some of the outer islands (the general manager estimates some 17 branches are unprofitable). All banks except BRED charge fees on accounts.

Despite the debacle of Vanuatu's failed Development Bank in the 1990s, a new Agricultural Development Bank opened its doors in March 2008. There is considerable skepticism in the marketplace as to how it might operate sustainably.

In addition, AusAID launched an Enterprise Challenge Fund in March 2008 to help fund higher-risk projects that might directly help with poverty reduction. Participating entrepreneurs are required to put up 50 percent of the funding for the venture.

Collateral Is a Key Problem in Accessing Credit, Especially for Women

Lack of acceptable collateral has been identified by firms in Vanuatu as the key reason for their limited access to credit (PEDF 2003). It is not uncommon in Vanuatu for banks to require a 100 percent offsetting cash deposit as security for a loan. No legislation in Vanuatu prevents women from owning property, nor is there any formal restriction on credit availability for women. But, as noted in the chapter on land, property in traditional communities is considered to be a male domain, and women are much less likely than men to have access to land title, making it more difficult for them to obtain credit.

A New Law May Improve the Collateral Situation for Women

The Financial Institutions Act No 2 of 1999, amended by Act No 21 of 2002, provides for the regulation of the business of banking in Vanuatu and for the licensing and supervision of financial institutions conducting banking business in the country.

With support from the Asian Development Bank, Vanuatu has recently enacted a new best-practice personal property secured transactions law, based on the New Zealand model. The new law provides a streamlined system for the creation, registration, protection, and prioritization of trans-actions secured by property other than land. This means that models of lending using a variety of forms of personal property as collateral should now become easier in Vanuatu. The legal framework now exists for using nonland assets as security for a loan. Credit Corporation (Vanuatu) Limited, a financing house based in Papua New Guinea, has already begun business in Vanuatu, having introduced such products into Fiji and well as Papua New Guinea.

The new legal framework has the potential to be of particular benefit to women, who are less likely than men to have access to land that could be used as collateral for loans. The challenge now is to introduce an electronic registry to support the new legislation and to ensure that information on the benefits of the new system are widely disseminated in Vanuatu, especially to women.

Lack of a Credit Reference System Means That Women Cannot Benefit from Good Repayment Rates

Vanuatu's poor ranking in the *Doing Business* indicators can be explained to a large extent by the lack of any formal credit reference system (table 4.1). No public or private credit rating agency as yet operates in Vanuatu.

Both VANWODS and formal banks have noted the excellent repayment rates achieved by their female customers. But in the absence of any formal credit reference system, women have limited ability to benefit from these repayment rates. In the character-based lending environment of Vanuatu, loans are skewed toward men. NBV's character-based lending through chiefs' recommendations, for example, results in only 15 percent

Table 4.1   Getting Credit—Benchmarking in the *Doing Business* Index

Indicator	Vanuatu	Region	OECD
Legal rights index[a]	8	5.8	6.8
Credit information index[b]	0	2.0	4.8
Public registry coverage (% adults)	0	7.2	8.4
Private bureau coverage (% adults)	0	11.3	58.4

Source: World Bank 2008.
a. The index ranges from 0 to 10, with higher scores indicating that those laws are better designed to expand access to credit.
b. This index measures the scope, access, and quality of credit information available through public registries or private bureaus. It ranges from 0 to 6, with higher values indicating that more credit information is available from a public registry or private bureau.

of loans going to women. Banks interviewed during the team missions in 2008 noted their willingness to provide larger loans to proven female borrowers, many of whom take out education loans, but women's lack of awareness about this fact means few are likely to take advantage of this opportunity. It may be sensible to consider developing a credit reference agency on a regional basis, in view of the economies of scale that a regional operation would generate.

Financial Literacy and Business Knowledge Matter

Access to finance is also dependent upon education levels and financial literacy. Many ni-Vanuatu are not familiar with modern banking services, and women in particular consider interest rates high and find products confusing.[5]

Local populations have relatively low financial literacy and limited income-generating opportunities and are further constrained by obligations to follow traditional *kastom* requirements to support extended family. Banks are trying to find relevant solutions. For example, Westpac has designed a basic financial literacy course, including budget planning, and translated it into local languages. Loans are being made against the new seasonal worker scheme in New Zealand described in chapter 7, coupled with practical money management training.

VANWODS management sees a large unmet need for financial literacy, business training, and better understanding of banking products for its members.[6] VANWODS staff noted in interviews that many of their members are running losses in their business, and having to ask husbands or relatives for funds to help repay their microfinance loans. A small survey of 124 Santo members of VANWODS found that 36 percent of them are making a loss in their business but are unaware of this fact because they do not keep proper records of sales and expenditures.[7]

Recommendations

- In the development of a regional credit bureau through the IFC's Financial Markets Infrastructure Program, support the collection of sex-disaggregated data.
- Support the recommendations of the UN Financial Services Sector Assessment to promote a regional program of support for expanding the reach of financial services, including innovative new partnerships, such as that between VANWODS and NBV on the outer islands, and

new products and delivery channels, such as mobile phone banking once the telecommunications infrastructure is upgraded.

- Expedite implementation of the new Personal Property Secured Transactions Act and the establishment of a new electronic registry to support it.
- Investigate with commercial banks and financial houses the potential to develop relevant new products in line with the Personal Property Secured Transactions Act and undertake outreach programs associated with the new law, especially those aimed at women.
- Provide financial literacy training for women borrowers, as well as training on how to write a bankable business plan.

Notes

1. Vanuatu Financial Services Commission. "Overview of Vanuatu's Financial Sector." http://www.vfsc.vu/offshore.html.
2. Interview conducted in April 2008.
3. Interview with NBV general manager, Bob Hughes, April 2008.
4. Interview with representatives of the National Provident Fund, April 2008.
5. Interviews and focus groups conducted in Port Vila, Santo, and Tanna in February and April 2008.
6. Interview with VANWODS managing director John Salong, April 2008.
7. Interview with Robyn Aburn, at the Santo VANWODS center, March 6, 2008.

CHAPTER 5

Enforcing Contracts

[C]hiefs and traditional leaders are responsive to the idea of women's rights (or respect for women), when couched in appropriate, non-confrontational language. However, ignorance of individual rights principles is widespread, and the authority of the constitution and of chiefs is often seen as in tension, rather than complementary.

The Unfinished State: Drivers of Change in Vanuatu
(Cox and others 2007)

Like many other processes associated with doing business in Vanuatu, contract enforcement in the formal system is costly. Vanuatu is ranked 67th out of 181 economies for contract enforcement (figure 5.1). As table 5.1 shows, the key problem is the cost of enforcing a contract through the Supreme Court. Because women are the most impoverished members of Vanuatu society, costly legal procedures render justice inaccessible to many ni-Vanuatu women. The Supreme Court has a backlog of about 1,000 cases, mostly commercial matters, including many land disputes (FIAS 2007).

Contract enforcement has recently been set back following the burning down of the court building in Port Vila and the consequent loss of all the court's records. In an effort to reduce the cost of contract

Figure 5.1   Enforcing Contracts—Vanuatu and Comparator Economies

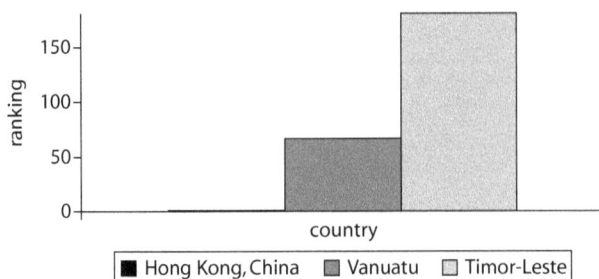

Source: World Bank 2008.

Table 5.1   Enforcing Contracts—Comparative Rankings

Indicator	Vanuatu	Region	OECD
Procedures (number)	30	37.2	30.8
Duration (days)	430	551	462.7
Cost (% of claim)	74.7	48.4	18.9

Source: World Bank 2008.

enforcement and to make the system more efficient and effective, the IFC is supporting the judiciary with the introduction of alternative dispute resolution mechanisms.

Women and the Traditional Justice System

Vanuatu has two legal systems operating simultaneously: the formal legal system (figure 5.2) and the customary system comprising customary rules and dispute resolution procedures, which vary across the country. The *Doing Business* indicators for contract enforcement consider cases heard in the Supreme Court. However, only a minority of disputes are dealt with in this forum. The vast majority of disputes are dealt with either in the lower courts (magistrates or Island Courts) or informally by chiefs.

In rural areas formal courts may be available only sporadically, when the courts go on circuit. Rural residents have no option, therefore, but to rely on chiefs to settle disputes. The vast majority of chiefs are men, and women are rarely called as experts at the *nakamal* (village court), although they are frequently considered the carriers and sustainers of custom from one generation to the next. Chiefs are not subject to any formal accountability mechanisms.

Figure 5.2   Formal Legal Jurisdiction over Civil Disputes

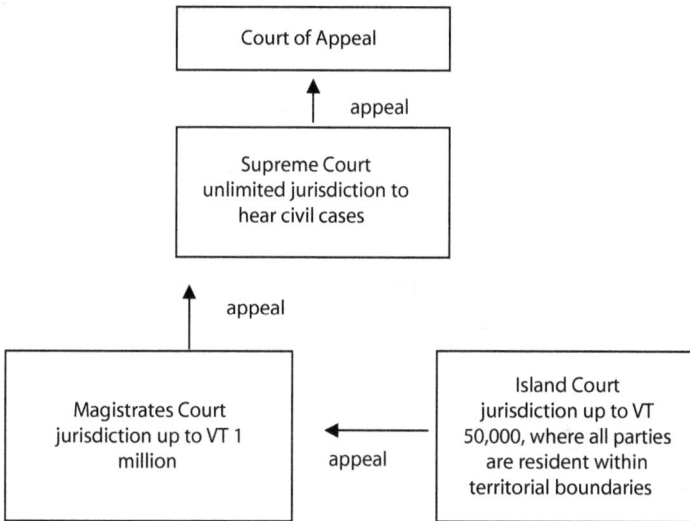

Court of Appeal

↑ appeal

Supreme Court
unlimited jurisdiction to
hear civil cases

↑ appeal

Magistrates Court
jurisdiction up to VT 1
million

← appeal

Island Court
jurisdiction up to VT
50,000, where all parties
are resident within
territorial boundaries

Source: Authors' depiction.

As women increasingly run their own businesses and become success-ful, they are more likely to become involved in disputes. Chapter 3 included an example of successful businesswomen on the island of Tanna who found that their land rights came into dispute as others noted their success and tried to profit from it. More women are using the formal sys-tem and the formal law and are avoiding custom courts because they think they will not get justice there (Jalal 1998). This problem was rec-ognized as early as 1994, when the chief justice proclaimed during the conference on violence and the family that "custom is failing ni-Vanuatu women" (Jolly 1996).

However, the most accessible courts in the formal system, the Island Courts, also dispense traditional justice, with each court having at least three justices knowledgeable in customary law, one of whom must be a "custom chief" from the region covered by the court. Article 45 of Vanuatu's constitution states that Island Courts should decide matters "wherever possible in conformity with custom," and Section 10 of the Island Court Act provides that "an island court shall administer the cus-tomary law prevailing within the territorial jurisdiction of the court so far as the same is not in conflict with any written law and is not contrary to justice, morality and good order."

Moreover, the legal profession is male dominated. None of Vanuatu's Court of Appeal or Supreme Court judges are female, although there are women magistrates. Only a few female lawyers practice in Vanuatu. There are a number of legal advice centers, some of which are aimed specifically at women, such as the Vanuatu Women's Center. They offer free legal advice in relation to domestic violence and child abuse, but rarely address business issues.

IFC's Commercial Mediation program is supporting the introduction of mediation into Vanuatu's dispute resolution system, enabling commercial cases to be resolved more quickly and cost effectively than is normally the case through formal court proceedings. This presents an opportunity to engage more women in the resolution of dispute resolution processes.

Recommendation

- Within the framework of the IFC's alternative dispute resolution procedures, train female mediators and run a public awareness campaign on the benefits of mediation, including a component of the campaign that targets female entrepreneurs.

CHAPTER 6

Employing Workers

[I]t is the wife who is expected to use her salary to feed the family, pay school fees and all household expenses, while the man considers his salary as his own for his own use in kava bars.

Office of the Prime Minister 2004

On measures of the ease of hiring and firing employees in the formal economy, Vanuatu is ranked 86th out of 181 economies (figure 6.1 and table 6.1). The key issue is the cost of firing workers, with a maximum of 56 weeks of salary payable.[1]

But only 16,300, or 14.7 percent, of Vanuatu's workers are formally employed—the lowest level in the Pacific region—and these workers are mainly concentrated in urban areas. In rural areas only 10 percent of the workforce is in paid employment (Cox and others 2007). Women provide major inputs into the informal economy in rural areas. As the government described in its 2004 report on CEDAW: "Women's participation in the garden tops the list of their otherwise traditional household related responsibilities and they participate in virtually all farming activities from ground preparation, planting, weeding, harvesting and post harvesting. These jobs are strenuous, labor intensive and time consuming" (Office of the Prime Minister 2004).

Figure 6.1   Employing Workers—Vanuatu and Comparator Economies

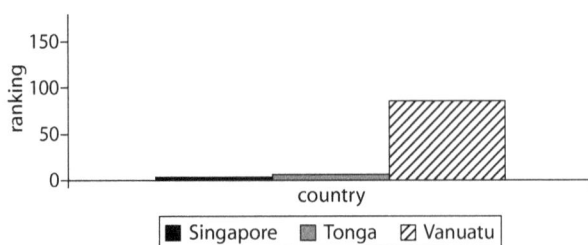

Source: World Bank 2008.
Note: Y axis is *Doing Business* ranking.

Table 6.1   Employing Workers—Comparative Rankings

Indicator	Vanuatu	Region	OECD
Difficulty of Hiring Index	22	19.2	25.7
Rigidity of Hours Index	40	19.2	42.2
Difficulty of Firing Index	10	20	26.3
Rigidity of Employment Index	24	19.5	31.4
Firing cost (weeks of wages)	56	38.6	25.8

Source: World Bank 2008.
Note: Each index assigns values between 0 and 100, with higher values representing more regulations. The Rigidity of Employment Index is an average of the three preceding indexes.

In the informal sector, women work predominantly as open-air vendors and handicraft makers and sellers, running stalls by the road side and at the markets (figure 6.2). Workers in the informal sector are disadvantaged because they are not covered by legislation and regulations. They do not receive sick leave, maternity leave, workers' compensation, or pensions. Employment contracts are usually not documented, abuse of employees is common, and recourse to the courts is difficult. Although both men and women suffer these hardships, women are especially disadvantaged because they make up such a large portion of the informal economy.

Women in the Formal Economy

Women are increasingly entering the formal economy as employees. The government's 2000 labor market survey shows that female employment had increased to about one-third of all employees in the formal sector, up from 27 percent in 1983. Moreover, data on poor people in the workforce indicate that women make up 36 percent of those working for pay or profit (figure 6.3).

Figure 6.2   Participation in the Informal Sector by Industry and Gender, 2000

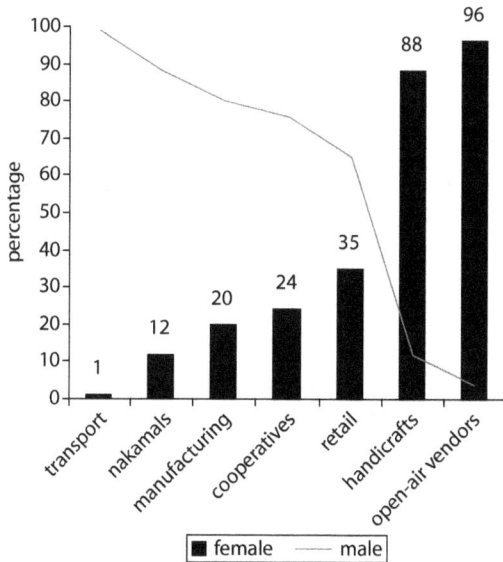

Source: Vanuatu Statistics Office 2000.

Figure 6.3   Poor People in the Workplace: Type of Work

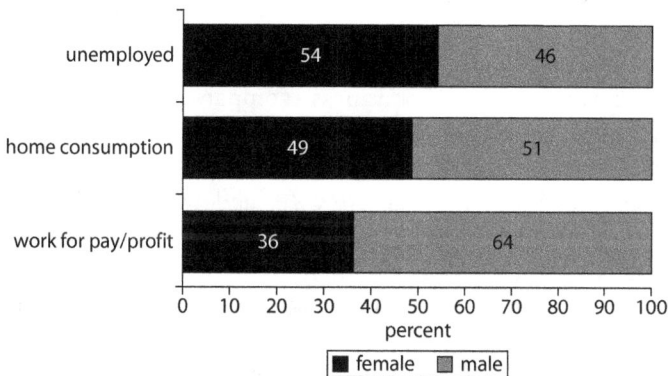

Source: Vanuatu Statistics Office 2006.

Yet, as noted in the CEDAW report, when both husband and wife work, "it is the wife who is expected to use her salary to feed the family, pay school fees and all household expenses, while the man considers his salary as his own for his own use in kava bars" (Office of the Prime Minister 2004).

Women's Employment Tends to Be in Traditional Roles

The 2002 labor market survey showed that female employment tends to be concentrated in certain categories: professional, technicians, and associate professionals (largely public sector workers); clerks, and service; and sales workers. Males dominate all categories, apart from clerks and service and sales workers.

Many women work as domestic servants (*haosgels*); in 1999 nearly 1,500 women held such jobs. Vanuatu has not signed the International Labour Organization's (ILO) convention on domestic workers, which is aimed at establishing working condition standards that are applicable to home workers.

Women Are Benefiting from a New Seasonal Employment Program in New Zealand

In 2007 the New Zealand government introduced a pilot program to use seasonal workers from Pacific island states to pick fruit and work on farms and vineyards. In 2008 about 1,300 ni-Vanuatu workers traveled to New Zealand on this program, and their earnings of approximately VT 7 million were repatriated to Vanuatu. Women from a number of the provinces, including Tanna and Epi, were part of this program. In the recent intake of 900 workers to New Zealand, roughly a third were estimated to be women.[2] In addition to wages and the potential for significant remittances, workers gain valuable on-the-job training in farming operations and food technologies and much needed exposure to farming as a commercial business (compared with the subsistence farming that is prevalent in Vanuatu). The development aspects of labor programs are highly regarded, and additional training is being considered after a trial in Otago, New Zealand, where workers attended night and weekend courses in computer technology and mechanics. It is possible that future workers might receive training in hospitality, business, and financial skills. Similar schemes are currently being considered in Australia.[3]

But traditional gender roles mean that fewer women are participating in the programs than might otherwise be the case. The number of women sent from each island depends on the individual community, which decides who will participate from that community. Some communities are supportive of women's participation, whereas others refuse to let female members go because of concerns over the erosion of community structures and traditional understandings about women's roles. Encouraging women's participation in the programs will be vital if ni-Vanuatu women are to enjoy equal access and benefits from this opportunity to develop skill and potentially commercial ventures.

The Law Prohibits Workplace Discrimination

Section 10 of Vanuatu's penal code contains far-reaching provisions, making it an offense to "discriminate against another person with respect to his right to the supply of goods or services, or to gain or continue in any employment, or to be admitted to any public place, by reason of the sex, ethnic or racial origin, or the religion of such other person." There do not appear to have been any prosecutions under this section. In addition, Vanuatu is the only country in the South Pacific with an employment law in effect that grants women the right to equal pay for equal work. Section 8 of this law states: "If a woman and man are doing similar work in the same organization, they should receive similar rates of pay. A woman is regarded as doing the same work as a man if her work is the same or broadly similar and if any difference between the things she does and the things he does are not of practical importance in relation to terms and conditions of employment." The law also prohibits forced labor and sex discrimination in employment. As noted in chapter one, women in the formal sector have slightly higher average salaries than men.

Benefits for Women in the Formal Economy

Vanuatu's benefits for workers in the formal economy are generous. The Employment Act provides for maternity pay for a 12-week period, which is less than the ILO's recommended standard of 14 weeks (box 6.1). Contrary to the ILO's recommendation, the employer is mandated to cover maternity pay; there is no subsidy from the government. Furthermore, women are eligible for maternity leave upon their hiring. Even women entrepreneurs have pointed out that this requirement can operate as disincentive for employing women. A minimum period of employment before becoming eligible for maternity benefits and a return-to-work provision could be proposed to overcome these concerns.

Annual leave and sick leave are also provided. The Employment Act provides for annual leave and sick leave for full-time employees, to be granted after 12 months of consecutive employment. The provisions are generous, although they do not cover casual and part-time workers.

Box 6.1

Maternity and Child Care Provisions in Vanuatu

- An employer shall allow a woman employee to leave her work upon production by her of a medical certificate stating that her confinement is likely to take place within 6 weeks, and shall not permit her to work during the 6 weeks following her confinement.
- While absent from work [on maternity leave] a woman employee shall be entitled to be paid not less than half of the remuneration she would have earned had she not been so absent.
- An employer shall allow a woman employee who is nursing a child half an hour twice a day during her working hours for this purpose; such interruptions of work shall be counted as working hours and shall be remunerated accordingly.
- Employers must make appropriate sanitary arrangements and wherever possible arrangements for breast feeding and other care of employees' young children.

The annual leave is calculated at one day for each month employed, and each employee is eligible for 21 days of sick leave. Some employers have reportedly dismissed workers before the 12-month qualification period to avoid having to pay for annual and sick leave.

Nearly 40 percent of all government employees are women. However, they tend to be employed at the lower end of the pay scale and on average earn only 80 percent of male public servant's salaries (Office of the Prime Minister 2004). Female public servants are granted maternity leave on full pay for 12 weeks. But only permanent and full-time staff are eligible for this benefit and for protection against discrimination in the workplace, excluding many women who are employed on a casual or part-time basis.

The National Provident Fund Provides for a Pension for All Workers in the Formal Economy

The Public Service Act as amended in 2001 requires employers and employees each to contribute 4 percent of their salary to the fund. In 2007, 7,790 women out of a total of 21,077 workers contributed to the fund (Vanuatu National Provident Fund 2007). Clearly women and men in the informal sector do not have access to such services, which effectively act as a form of superannuation savings.

Strengthening Employment Rights

An employment relations bill that would strengthen and expand many of the current benefits that women have was drafted in 2005 but had not been passed as of early 2009. Some of its provisions, however, were incorporated into an Employment Act Amendment, passed by Parliament in November 2008.

The current employment law nonetheless still includes some discriminatory provisions, such as barring women from working at night except under certain conditions and in certain jobs such as nursing and the hospitality industry. The current law should be amended to remove such restrictions.

Recommendation

• Pass another amendment to the Employment Act to address the night-working provisions for women.

Notes

1. After 12 months of service, an employee who is fired is entitled to half a month's pay for each year of service. See Section 56 of the Employment Act of 1988.

2. Interview with John Capper, New Zealand High Commission, April 24, 2008.

3. Hamish McDonald, "Rich and Poor Share a Harvest of Plenty," *Sydney Morning Herald*, April 28, 2008, p. 1.

CHAPTER 7

Trading across Borders

The level of understanding of trade issues is rudimentary and therefore some form of basic training of selected trade issues for women in business would be beneficial.

Integrated Framework 2007

Facilitating trade is vital to achieving broad-based growth in Vanuatu. Because of the country's small size and the overcrowded nature of the domestic market for locally produced goods, international trade offers a much needed outlet for private sector growth and economic development. It also offers the potential to create income-earning opportunities in rural enterprises, where the majority of ni-Vanuatu women are engaged.

Yet Vanuatu is by far the most costly country in the Pacific in which to conduct international trade. "Trading across Borders" is Vanuatu's poorest performing indicator in the World Bank's *Doing Business* survey, where the country ranked 136th of 181 countries in 2008 (table 7.1). Exports and imports commonly travel by sea in the Pacific, and Vanuatu's archipelago creates particular challenges for the distribution of goods. Interisland shipping is unreliable and infrequent, though this is a problem common to many Pacific island countries. Even where export

Table 7.1   Trading across Borders—Comparative Rankings

Indicator	Vanuatu	Region	OECD
Documents for export (number)	7	6.7	4.5
Time for export (days)	26	23.3	10.7
Cost to export (US$ per container)	1,497	902.3	1,069.1
Documents for import (number)	9	7.1	5.1
Time for import (days)	30	24.5	11.4
Cost to import (US$ per container)	1,392	948.5	1,132.7

Source: World Bank 2008.

commodities are produced and delivered efficiently, the high cost of shipping prohibits goods from reaching global markets at a competitive price. High-value or time-sensitive goods are typically transported by airfreight (AusAID 2008), but while the 2004 entry of the Virgin Blue subsidiary Pacific Blue has lowered costs and increased passenger traffic, high airfreight charges on exports remain unchanged. Given the dependence of much of the population on the production of agriculture, port costs significantly constrain the ability of ni-Vanuatu to participate in the global commodity market and ultimately reduce farm-gate prices.

These challenges to trading affect both male and female entrepreneurs, but they often have a greater impact on women. A comprehensive trade diagnostic study of Vanuatu found that the issue of women in trade has been given some ad hoc attention through training programs for business-women and through a small loans facility. The study noted that the level of understanding of trade issues in Vanuatu's government is rudimentary and that some form of basic training in selected trade issues for women in business would be beneficial (Integrated Framework 2007).

Vanuatu's Trade Profile

Agricultural commodities continue to form the majority of goods exports in Vanuatu, although their relative shares vary depending on weather conditions and global demand. Kava, a traditional medicine used throughout Pacific societies as an analgesic, tranquilizer, and antidepressant, has been a valuable export for Vanuatu, although restrictions on its importation by Australia and several European countries due to health concerns dampened demand in 2007. Continued strong demand in the Pacific islands for Vanuatu's high-quality product should ease the effect of those restrictions to some extent. Men predominate in kava production, and the few women who have tried to break into the sector have faced challenges. The Vanuatu Commodities Marketing Board has established a monopoly over the export of agricultural products, including kava. The marketing board purchases dried kava from farmers at VT 1,000 per kilogram, well below the production cost, while selling to a monopoly supplier in the lucrative New Caledonian market at VT 2,700, running a monopoly business at the expense of individual farmers (Cox and others 2007).

Tourism, Which Generates Income for Large Numbers of Women, Is Increasingly Driving Economic Growth

The strong Australian dollar (around 53 percent of tourists originate from Australia[1]) and the rise in the number of airlines servicing Vanuatu have led to increasing numbers of tourists. 2007 revenues from tourism earnings were likely to be in excess of the VT 11,000 million forecast in mid-2007, about three times the size of earnings from goods exports (table 7.2). Tourism now accounts for about 18 percent of GDP.[2] Real GDP growth in tourism and travel is expected to average 6.8 percent over the coming 10 years.[3] Given the disproportionate representation of women in the tourism industry, increased tourism is likely to encourage broad-based economic growth over the longer term, although tourism remains strongest on the main island of Efate and hence most of the gains will be found in urban and peri-urban areas. Tourism has only limited spillover to the other major islands (box 7.1), which remain dependent on subsistence farming and small-scale agriculture.

With Vanuatu a Regular Cruise Ship Stopover, Tourism Could Offer Large Potential for Women's Handicrafts

Women make up 88 percent of the handicrafts industry and 96 percent of open-air vendors catering to tourists (Vanuatu Statistics Office 2000). Yet their products tend to be poorly developed and do not appeal to the tourist market. Products sold include colorful island dresses, jewelry made of beads, and purses made out of local grasses. Numerous copycat businesses lead women to compete against each other for a small market. Moreover, women complain that the local market is being flooded by island dresses made in China. With no legislation in place to protect traditional skills, women are demanding the protection of their cultural heritage through intellectual property laws.

Table 7.2   Current Account Balance, 2005–07
(millions of vatu)

Category	2005 actual	2006 revised	2007 forecast
Current account balance	−2,379	−3,466	−5,100
Trade (Goods) Balance	−10,178	−12,130	−13,000
Exports[a]	4,166	4,166	4,000
of which Copra	126	347	300
Beef	301	318	300
Cocoa	181	318	300
Kava	477	656	300
Coconut oil	732	146	200
Imports[a]	−14,344	−16,296	−17,000
Services	6,087	8,207	8,500
Credit	14,145	16,088	16,500
(of which tourism earnings)	8,314	10,185	11,000
Debit	−8,058	−7,881	−8,000
Investment income	−2,728	−2,343	−4,100
Credit	3,032	3,521	3,900
Debit	−5,760	−5,864	−8,000
Current transfers (net)	4,440	2,800	3,500

Source: Reserve Bank of Vanuatu 2007.
a. Exports and imports figure are given free on board.

Box 7.1

Case Study: Ecotourism on Tanna Island

Tanna Evergreen Bungalows is a "dream come true" for husband-and-wife team Sam and Meriane Numake. Conducting driving tours around Tanna for tourists and visitors back in 1995, Sam and Meriane noticed the construction work beginning on Tanna's new airport. The couple decided to acquire a picturesque piece of land to set up a boutique resort for island visitors. "We saw the potential of establishing accommodation close to the airport and in 1996, commenced building. It took two years to establish a small restaurant, four modest shared-facilities bungalows, and one touring vehicle," says Meriane. Today, the business also offers activities such as volcano tours, horse-riding safaris, and snorkeling.

The resort regularly has full occupancy, but lack of capital is a constraint to further business growth. Because of the challenge ni-Vanuatu women face in obtaining credit, Meriane came up with her share of the start-up capital by approaching four family members to be shareholders. The rest came from her savings in the National Provident Fund. In 2003, when the pair expanded the business, Meriane

(continued)

Box 7.1 *(Continued)*

managed to secure a loan from the bank, but since then it has been more difficult to obtain loans. According to Meriane, the banks constantly make up excuses for not granting her loans, even though her experience in a cooperative company has taught her how to run a business and she knows her business plan is sound.

The couple has also had problems ensuring their guests a regular supply of electricity, which the business obtains from a generator. The generator operates for around 8 hours a day, but is inadequate for overseas tourists who expect constant power. Their bungalow business has prevailed despite these challenges. "We are now the largest 100 percent-owned and -operated ni-Vanuatu bungalow on Tanna Island and have won the Best Bungalow of the Year in 2006 at the Vanuatu Hospitality Awards," Meriane says. Sam and Meriane put their success down to their self-reliance, "our greatest motivation," and the couple will continue to apply for loans. "We want to encourage other ni-Vanuatus to work for themselves and ensure their country's economic independence."

In Port Vila women have organized themselves into the Centrepoint Market Women's Association, which attempts to organize women who sell handicrafts. The association, which has 72 members, is housed in a building close to the port; women buy stalls there from which to sell their goods, but the association does not appear able to offer its members many benefits or to serve as an effective advocacy body.

To help expose the women to other markets and ideas, the Chamber of Commerce prides itself on the number of women it has sponsored at trade shows (in New Caledonia, for example). Yet the women could benefit from much more extensive training and advice on diversifying their products and expanding the range and quality, as well as on adapting their traditional products to the taste of the tourist market.

Women Play a Significant Role in Fishing Activities, But They Are Rarely Involved in Exporting Fish

According to the Vanuatu Statistics Office (2007), 77 percent of households were engaged in some form of fishing activity in 2006. Large numbers of ni-Vanuatu women gather fish and shellfish for home consumption and are involved in preservation, marketing, and distribution of fish, and increasingly also in artisanal fishing (Commonwealth Secretariat, undated).

Yet women are rarely involved in fish export activities, which remain the domain of men. Frozen fish accounted for 49 percent of commodity exports in 2005. Little of this is likely to have benefited women, as they are usually not the recipients of such income, according to a trade brief prepared by the World Bank in 2008. The government has worked to develop marine exports, yet women's involvement in this process has been negligible. Given women's strong but largely invisible contribution to fishing, supporting their role in the development of future programs and interventions would be beneficial to the overall development of the sector.

Vanuatu's Participation in Trade Liberalization

Vanuatu is covered by several trade arrangements and has entered or is entering into negotiations on two others. In February 2008 Vanuatu completed the domestic requirements to be able to trade under the terms and conditions of Pacific Island Countries Trade Agreement, joining five other countries committed to liberalizing their goods markets by 2021.[4] Vanuatu is also a member of the Melanesian Spearhead Group, which also includes Fiji, New Caledonia, Papua New Guinea, and the Solomon Islands.

Negotiations for the European Partnership Agreement (EPA) commenced in 2002 when the existing Cotonou Agreement was found to be noncompliant with World Trade Organization (WTO) standards. The agreement was scheduled to be completed by December 2007, but only two Pacific island countries—Fiji and Papua New Guinea—had signed by that date, with no other agreement finalized. The European Union was wary of giving concessions to Pacific island countries that it would then also have to give to Africa and the Caribbean, the two other EPA partner regions. Discussions with its negotiating partner, the Pacific Island Forum Secretariat, broke down into acrimony as the December 2007 deadline approached, and a resolution of the impasse does not appear to be imminent.

PACER Plus Is Likely to Offer the Greatest Benefits to Pacific Island Countries, Given Their Close Trading Relationship with Australia and New Zealand

Partially in response to the EPA negotiations, the Pacific Agreement on Closer Economic Relations (PACER) between Australia, New Zealand, and the 14 Forum Island Countries (FICs) came into force in 2003. This is a framework agreement, rather than a regional trade agreement, designed to gradually integrate the economies of the FICs with

Australia and New Zealand. Australia and New Zealand already offer duty- and quota-free access to all FICs under the 1981 South Pacific Regional Trade and Economic Cooperation Agreement, but the agreement is nonreciprocal and PACER was designed to direct FICs toward a WTO-compliant regional trade agreement—PACER Plus. Negotiations for PACER Plus are likely to begin by 2010 and will include negotiations on services, foreign direct investment, and the movement of persons.

Vanuatu Has Also Signaled That It Plans to Recommence Its Stalled WTO Accession

A Diagnostic Trade Integration Study, which was undertaken through the Integrated Framework program in late 2007, appears to have been the impetus for a renewed engagement with the WTO, and the accession process is now being discussed again—more than a decade after it began.[5] The accession process stalled in 2001, at the nadir of Vanuatu's economic downturn. Because agreement had been reached on goods and service schedules, the accession process will be straightforward if Vanuatu chooses to go ahead.

The Government Has Only a Limited Understanding of Gender and Trade Issues in Vanuatu

The same diagnostic study noted "a lack of understanding in Vanuatu's Department of Women's Affairs of how the various trade arrangements can be used to benefit women in business whether in the informal or formal sector." While the Vanuatu National Council of Women has sought greater participation in the discussions of regional and international trade agreements, the Trade Department has not engaged with the council in trade discussions.

As well as liberalization under regional and multilateral trade arrangements, unilateral liberalization of services is proving successful for Vanuatu and having positive effects on women. Liberalization in international aviation services has had a dramatic impact on the tourism industry, with liberalization of routes between Australia and Vanuatu resulting in an almost 20 percent increase in visitor arrivals in the subsequent year (figure 7.1). Given the predominance of women in the tourism sector, both in low-paying jobs and in tourism management, this liberalization is likely to have created a substantial number of new economic opportunities for women (box 7.2). The telecommunications market, liberalized early in 2008, likewise has the potential to

Figure 7.1   Percentage Increase in Passenger Traffic in the Year Following Entry of New Airlines

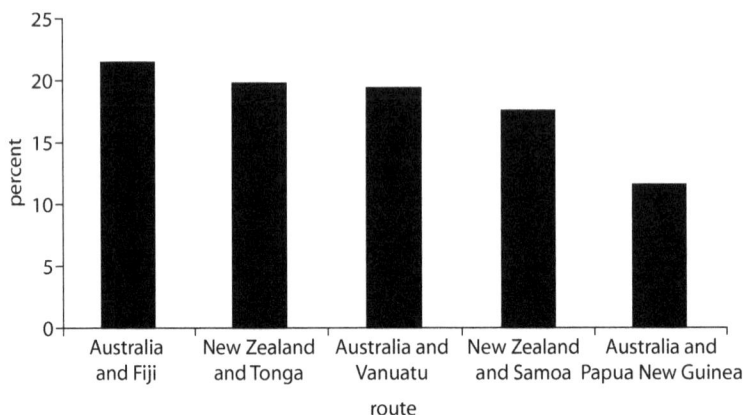

Source: AusAID 2008.

Box 7.2

Women's Businesses Benefiting from Tourism: Lapita Café

Vatansi Mackenzie always had an interest in cooking and healthy eating, but she did not turn it into a business until she lost her job following a strike. While still employed, Vatansi sold snacks on the side, and after losing her job, she decided to cook and serve local foods full time. "We have an emerging problem here in Vanuatu with communicable diseases, so I decided to promote local foods as they are organic and healthy," she says. Vatansi opened Lapita Café in 1999 but closed it following a recession and decided to focus instead on commercial catering, using the same business name. She sells her products in local supermarkets and caters for university and government functions.

Her business really took off when Air Vanuatu decided to make her the supplier for their in-flight snacks. "It took me four years to get that contract," she says. "But I kept courting them." She has been supplying snacks such as cookies and banana chips for the airline's regional flights since 2002 and currently provides about 6,000 bags of banana chips a week. Vatansi employs seven staff in the kitchen and the office. According to her, "a lot of women are involved in this kind of production but on a smaller scale."

Going forward, she is looking to expand to New Caledonia and experimenting with how best to improve the shelf life of her products. She would also like to improve her product packaging to include nutritional information and better labeling.

improve the welfare and economic opportunities of women, as has been the case in other countries.[6]

Addressing Trade Challenges

Vanuatu faces a number of significant challenges in seeking to expand its international trade. Ni-Vanuatu farmers, for example, continue to export agricultural commodities in predominantly raw or unprocessed farm exports that bring lower returns than those for processed goods (Bazely and Mullen 2006). Persisting with this approach offers limited potential for small-scale farmers to benefit from international trade. "Upgrading"— moving further up the value chain by integrating more lucrative components of production where fewer competitors exist—offers a way for small-scale agricultural commodity exporters to develop and grow their enterprise (Kaplinsky 2006). Upgrading can involve processing raw products close-to-source, such as drying and baking fruit to make dried fruits or chips or processing berries and fruits to make jam.[7] Higher-value commodities such as vanilla, spices, nuts, sandalwood and tamanu oil, and high-quality cocoa and coffee also hold significant market potential for Vanuatu (Business Advantage 2008) and could attract a premium if they were certified, using organic or other quality certification systems. However, entry into these markets is undermined by the restrictive business environment, the challenge of achieving economies of scale, and other issues unique to certified organic agricultural production in the Pacific (AusAID 2008; Mapasua and Maccari 2007).

Organic and Fair Trade Certification Programs Could Improve Returns to Farmers by Moving Them Further Up the Value Chain

Certification programs have the potential to move producers up the value chain while also achieving social outcomes. In 2007 Australians spent $A 11 million on fair trade-certified products and were expected to spend over $A 20 million in 2008, according to the Fair Trade Association of Australia and New Zealand.

But certification programs remain poorly understood and accessed in the Pacific. Certification is costly and the process of attaining certification can be very difficult for small producers. There is also little awareness of the benefits of certification programs in Pacific island bureaucracies, and no policies exist to deliberately encourage market development despite the Forum Island Countries' regional strategy for agriculture and food security, which identifies certification as one way to facilitate product upgrading and access to niche markets (Mapasua and Maccari 2007). Nongovernmental organizations concerned with these matters are becoming more active in the Pacific and are partnering with small producers.

Fair Trade Principles Can Help Integrate Women and Marginalized Producers into International Markets

Fair trade principles target disadvantaged and marginalized producers and help them to access markets on terms and conditions respecting their interest and circumstances through the formation of producer organizations. When producers join a fair trade certification program, members receive a defined minimum price for their produce, and the organization receives a social premium for community development and infrastructural projects as well as prefinancing, capacity-building, and technical assistance from buyers with whom producers build long-term, direct-trading partnerships. Gender equality is a key fair trade principle, which ensures women's work is paid and valued equally and that women gain leadership, decision-making, and managerial positions within their cooperatives. There are some emerging success stories of using fair trade principles to develop women's handicrafts in Vanuatu, and the lessons might prove useful for replicating this approach in other sectors of regions of Vanuatu (box 7.3).

However, the existing fair trade certification system poses obstacles to Pacific producers' market entry (see for example Mapasua 2008). The

Box 7.3

Developing Fair Trade Handicrafts Markets

On Vanuatu's remote North Ambae island, weaving baskets from the leaves of the *pandanus* tree is a long tradition among women. The women would like to sell their baskets, but accessing markets has become increasingly difficult and untenable as a source of reliable income. To sell their baskets to gift shop suppliers, the weavers must walk four to six hours to the nearest major marketplace. Many Ambae women have in fact refused to learn weaving because of poor market access. Other obstacles that frustrated their business efforts included poor infrastructure (especially at ports); unreliable or no communications technology; shipping expenses and the high cost of some (imported) inputs; and a lack of banking services, access, and facilities.

(continued)

Box 7.3 *(Continued)*

Sandrine Wallez, a French expatriate living in Port Vila, had the idea for a fair trade shop in Port Vila that would buy and sell handicrafts made by rural women and men living in poverty in Vanuatu. At a Peace Corps conference in 2006, Wallez met Blake Stogner, a volunteer who heard Wallez speak about her idea to sell the women's baskets under fair trade conditions and decided to help her.

Establishing a trading partnership with the weavers on North Ambae was no easy task. With no standardized prices or certification and labeling system available for fair trade handicrafts, Stogner did a rough supply chain assessment to determine pricing, costing, and bag-sizing requirements. Even more challenging was the lack of education and business skills among women in North Ambae.

According to Stogner, "North Ambae is the 'worst-case scenario' we'll come across in Vanuatu. The women are particularly dispersed and disadvantaged. They are illiterate and have no basic numerical skills or training and no comprehension of product and trading requirements—things like product sizing and pricing. They've had bad experiences in selling—where relatives sell their bags in Vila but never send back any money. Ambae is also very mountainous—there's no transport infrastructure, so women walk for days in difficult conditions to get their goods to one central point."

Despite the challenges, the women on North Ambae have become well organized, and their weaving enterprise a success. Wallez' enterprise, World of Wonders, bought VT 280,000 ($A 3,100) worth of the women's products in 2006, and VT 470,000 ($A 5,200) in 2007. The group of 24 weavers on North Ambae island will soon rise to 50, and Wallez is expanding this pilot initiative to other island communities, including Ambrym, Efate, Erromango, Malekula, and Pentecost. The network now includes roughly 200 women weavers who stay within their communities while still engaging in trade. In addition to selling the women's goods domestically, Wallez is assisting them to access value added fair trade markets overseas.

Fairtrade Labelling Organizations International (FLO), the nonprofit body that sets fair trade standards, certifies producers, and provides producer support, needs to develop pricing requirements for fair trade products from the Pacific, and modify the international fair trade standards to suit the Pacific context (FairMatch Support 2008). FLO aims to address these limitations in the coming years (FLO 2008).

Incorporating as a Charitable Association May Be Necessary to Comply with the Requirements of Fair Trade

A charitable association is not generally regarded as a suitable vehicle for conducting a business in Vanuatu because it is not aimed at making a profit, but its structure may help Pacific-based entrepreneurs to support producers to access fair trade markets by complying with the current requirements of the World Fair Trade Organization (WFTO). The WFTO certifies fair trade organizations, which are committed to fair trade principles and operate in both producer and consumer countries.[8] To ensure that producers gain maximum benefit from the transaction, consumer country fair trade organizations purchase uncertified fair trade products from producer associations but not from individual enterprises. Incorporation as a charitable entity has in one case aimed to accommodate this requirement for small businesses run by women that are producing handicrafts and other household goods.

Recommendations

- Provide access to basic market training for women in the handicrafts industry, to help them diversify their products and improve product quality and design to better target the tourist market.
- Consider partnerships with tourist operators who have a vested interest in improving the quality of handicrafts.
- Provide information sessions and training to relevant regional and national bureaucracies on fair trade market opportunities and benefits.
- Provide financial assistance and in-country support to key fair trade organizations and networks.
- Fund further research on fair trade in Vanuatu and the Pacific to investigate barriers to small producers' and artisans' access to the fair trade certification system and alternative fair trade market opportunities.

Notes

1. Reserve Bank of Vanuatu (2007), p. 26.
2. DTIS (http://www.integratedframework.org/files/english/Vanuatu_concept_paper.pdf).
3. World Travel and Tourism Council. "Vanuatu Key Facts at a Glance" (http://www.wttc.org/eng/Tourism_Research/Tourism_Satellite_Accounting/TSA_Country_Reports/Vanuatu_/).

4. As of March 2008, these countries were Cook Islands, Fiji, Niue, Samoa, and the Solomon Islands.

5. Diagnostic Trade Integration Studies (DTIS) are designed to ensure that trade is mainstreamed into the national economic development process, based on a pro-poor strategy that relates growth to employment creation and human development.

6. See, for example, the case studies of Grameen Bank's village phone program in Bangladesh, where 95 percent of phone operators are female (http://www. digitaldividend.org/case/case_grameen.htm).

7. The most lucrative form of value-chain upgrading is own-brand manufacturing, because the trademark rights that underwrite brands offer ongoing (rather than temporary) protection from competition (Kaplinsky 2006).

8. The WFTO is currently piloting a new Sustainable Fair Trade Management System, which will provide producers of handicrafts and other goods with a product label to access mainstream commercial markets for their goods (IFAT 2008; Commons 2008).

Summary of Focus Group Discussions with Female Entrepreneurs in Vanuatu

As part of in-country research for this publication, the team conducted two focus group discussions with female entrepreneurs in Port Vila and on the island of Tanna. The consultations revealed that gender relations are not homogenous across Vanuatu, and neither are businesswomen's issues. For example, businesswomen in Port Vila discussed pitiable bank service, while women on Tanna noted a lack of access to finance. Businesswomen in Port Vila discussed their involvement in the lucrative kava bar industry, while women on Tanna are excluded from this traditionally male industry because of customary associations of kava with male fertility. The most striking observation from both groups is how willing and appreciative the businesswomen were to be consulted, because they so rarely are. Below is a summary of the main barriers to business development that the women raised, discussions of which have been incorporated throughout the text of this book:

- Women need *more affordable training* and advice to succeed in business. They asked for the following skills and training opportunities: advocacy, bargaining, stock control, financial management and investment services (managing value-added tax returns, how to invest money rather than just save), human resources, product development, sourcing markets (international and domestic), and legal knowledge about business rights and start-up requirements.

- Vanuatu women rarely ask for help and feel that they should take a back seat to men. Women are willing to learn but are reluctant to take training, especially if it costs money.
- A number of steps are required to start a business and involve different government departments that appear to operate as silos and can give conflicting advice. Women noted that often the business license fees and other *start-up requirements* to formalize a business are out of reach for them. These requirements are confusing, expensive, or time consuming. The women also complained that the government departments are not friendly to businesswomen and do not take them seriously. Women suggested a one-stop shop where all business processes could be managed or at least a place they felt comfortable going to for business information, financing options, and training opportunities.
- Women were interested in mentoring between successful businesswomen and those who are just starting out, and hoped for more networking and associations friendly to women.
- *Human resources* are a concern. Staff are poorly trained, have attitude problems and a poor work ethic, and lack customer service and other skills. Women expressed interest in business training to help train Pacific Islanders in customer service and for ni-Vanuatu businesses to learn how Australian and New Zealand businesses operate. The possibility of the Australian Pacific Technical College offering customer service certificates and courses in small business management and beauty therapy was raised. *Lack of education and illiteracy* are problems among the staff. Many businesswomen have to train their staff themselves.
- Rural women are less educated and struggle to understand business requirements.
- Men are meant to be patriarchs and sometimes feel emasculated when women are assertive. When considered too successful, women are often harassed by men and even by other women. As a result, women sometimes stop promoting and networking, hindering their business growth.
- *Access to finance* is a major issue for Tanna businesswomen. While microfinance and savings and loans schemes have been established, they are often used as a cash management system—women can only loan what they have saved and enjoy getting their cash "out of sight." Other women have withdrawn their superannuation to start businesses. Because land cannot be used as collateral, women can access

finance only through long-term savings. To put this into perspective, women will often save for 10 years before they can take out a loan.

— Many women told stories of banks denying women credit, perpetuating the belief that banks are frightening, untrustworthy, and unwelcoming to women.
— Women feel the 12 percent interest rate is too high.
— Many women felt that banks should be friendlier. They said they are not taken seriously as business owners and felt that banks need to explain their products better.
— Debt collectors should be regulated.

• Women expressed great need for improved *access to markets and product development*. Businesses compete with one another and produce similar goods. The women did not understand how to access international markets, unless they spent time in an advanced economy. Few used the Internet to access markets.
• A lack of *infrastructure* and crippling *utility costs* are barriers to business growth. Utilities are unreliable and it can take "forever" to get a phone connected, unless you have a family member or friend in a relevant department to expedite the process. Women on Tanna also mentioned the irregular supply of water and electricity to be problematic.
• *Transportation* and freight costs are seen as a barrier to business growth. Transportation from outlying islands to Port Vila is costly, and rising petrol prices make getting goods to market expensive. An inefficient port monopoly makes importing and exporting problematic. Lengthy and costly delays hurt businesses engaged in importing and exporting.
• *Security* incidents such as pillaging and stealing are increasing, adding to the costs of doing business. Women are often targeted, especially if alone.
• *Familial responsibilities* can hinder enterprise development. It is difficult for women to get ahead in business because there is pressure to support more family every time the business grows. For example, it is common for successful businesswomen to pay for their sibling children's school fees. Some businesswomen move away from extended family as a strategy for business growth.

— Family "credit" sends many small enterprises out of business.
— Men and family "need to understand what business means for a woman so they do not keep helping themselves" to her profits.

• *Land disputes* are an extremely common problem on the island of Tanna. They prevent women from expanding their businesses and from operating to full capacity. One woman explained that land owners were "jealous of her success" and so denied her access to the land she uses.

- Women who worked in *marketplaces* or sold food at stalls commented on the lack of shelter and areas designated for the sale of goods, forcing them to sell food at roadside stalls rather than under cover with proper sanitation facilities. Marketplaces require expansion to accommodate the women.
- There is need for some sort of alternative dispute resolution system or a small claims court to hear women's grievances in a cost-affordable manner.

References

ADB (Asian Development Bank). 2006. "Vanuatu 2006–2009, Country Strategy and Program Update." http://www.adb.org/Documents/CSPs/VAN/2006/csp-van-2006.pdf.

AusAID (Australian Agency for International Development). 2008. *Pacific Economic Survey, 2008*. Canberra.

Cox, Marcus, and others. 2007. *Unfinished State: Drivers of Change in Vanuatu*. Canberra: AusAID.

Bazely, P., and B. Mullen. 2006. "Vanuatu Economic Opportunities Fact-Finding Mission." Paper commissioned by AusAID, Canberra.

Bolton, Lissant. 1998. "Women Have Kastom Too: Changing the Definition of Kastom in Vanuatu." Department of Anthropology, Center for the Contemporary Pacific Research School of Pacific and Asian Studies, Australian National University, Canberra.

——. 2003. *Unfolding the Moon: Enacting Women's Kastom in Vanuatu*. Honolulu, University of Hawaii Press.

Business Advantage International Pty Ltd. 2008. "Business Advantage Vanuatu 2008." Melbourne. http://www.cmmc.com.au/vanuatu.shtml.

Commons, M. 2008. "Fair Trade Products and Supply Chain Certification. Consultation, Round One." *Organic Standard* 86 (June): 13–14.

Commonwealth Secretariat. Undated. "Women Act as Backbone of Fishing Activities in Vanuatu." London. http://www.genderandtrade.org/gtinformation/164419/169607/169608/women_fishing_pacific/.

Economist Intelligence Unit. 2007. *Vanuatu Country Profile*. London.

———. 2008. *Vanuatu Country Report 2008*. London.

ESCAP. 2007. *Economic and Social Survey of Asia and the Pacific 2007*. ESCAP, Bangkok.

FairMatch Support. 2008. "Pacific Growers Export Partnership PGEP," Version 1, August 11. Amersfoort, the Netherlands.

Fairtrade Labelling Organizations International (FLO). 2008. "Proposal to FLO Board of Directors on 'Fairtrade in Small Island Developing States (SIDs) in SE Asia and Oceania.'" Bonn, September 22.

FIAS (Foreign Investment Advisory Services). 2007. "Vanuatu: Mini-Diagnostic Analysis of the Investment Climate." World Bank, Washington, DC.

Hoddinott, J., and L. Haddad. 1995. "Does Female Income Share Influence Household Expenditures? Evidence from Côte d'Ivoire." *Oxford Bulletin of Economics and Statistics* 57: 77–96.

Integrated Framework for Trade Related Technical Assistance. 2007. "Vanuatu Diagnostic Trade Integration Study." vol. 1 draft. World Trade Organization, Geneva.

International Fair Trade Association (IFAT). 2008. "The Sustainable Fair Trade Management System." August version of "First Draft." Culemborg, the Netherlands.

Jalal, P. I. 1998. *Law for Pacific Women: A Legal Rights Handbook*. Fiji Women's Rights Movement, Suva.

Jolly, Margaret. 1994. *Women of the Place: Kastom, Colonialism, and Gender in Vanuatu*. London: Routledge.

———. 1996. "Woman Ikat Raet Long Human Raet O No?: Women's Rights, Human Rights and Domestic Violence in Vanuatu." *Feminist Review* 52: 169–90.

Kaplinsky, R. 2006. "How Can Agricultural Commodity Producers Appropriate a Greater Share of Value Chain Incomes?" In *Agricultural Commodity Markets and Trade: New Approaches to Analysing Market Structure and Instability*, ed. A. Sarris and D. Hallam. Cheltenham: Edward Elgar.

Lapi, G., and L. Jimmy. 2006. "A Review of the Education and Training of Women and Girls in Vanuatu." Paper prepared for the National Women's Forum. Port Vila.

Lunnay C, J. Fingleton, M. Mangawai, E. Nalyyal, and J. Simo. 2007. *Vanuatu: Review of National Land Legislation, Policy and Land Administration*. Canberra: AusAID.

Luthria, Manjula, and others. 2006. "At Home and Away: Expanding Job Opportunities for Pacific Islanders through Labor Mobility." World Bank, Washington, DC.

Mapasua, K. 2008. "Fair Trade in Samoa and the Pacific." Presentation at Fair Trade Association of Australia and New Zealand Annual General Meeting, Melbourne, August 27–28.

Mapasua, K., and M. Maccari, 2007. "An Overview of Organic Agriculture in the Pacific." International Federation of Organic Agriculture Movements, Bonn. http://www.ifoam.org/partners/projects/pdfs/OA_Pacific_web.pdf.

Molisa, Grace Mera. 1991. "The Politics of Difference: Feminism, Colonialism and Decolonisation in Vanuatu." In *Intersexions: Gender/Class/Culture/Ethnicity*, ed. G. Bottomley, M. de Lepervanche, and J. Martin, pp. 52–74. Sydney: Allen and Unwin.

Morrison, Andrew, Dhushyanth Raju, and Nistha Sindha. 2007. "Gender Equality, Poverty and Economic Growth." Policy Research Working Paper 4349. World Bank, Washington, DC.

Nari, Russell. 2000. "Land Tenure and Resource Management: A Major Challenge in Vanuatu." *Pacific Economic Bulletin* 15 (2). http://peb.anu.edu.au/pdf/peb15-2nari.pdf.

Naupa, A., and J. Simo. 2007. *Matrilineal Land Tenure in Vanuatu: Case Studies of Raga and Mele' in Matrilineal Land Tenure in the Marshall Islands, the Solomon Islands and Vanuatu.* Suva, Fiji: Pacific Forum Secretariat.

Naviti 2003. "Restorative Justice and Women in Vanuatu." In *A Kind of Mending: Restorative Justice in the Pacific Islands*, ed. S. Dinnen, pp. 265–74. Canberra: Pandanus Books.

Nichols, Shane. 2007. "VANWODS Microfinance, Impact Assessment." World Education Australia, St. Leonards.

Office of the Prime Minister and Department of Women's Affairs, Vanuatu. 2004. "Combined Initial, Second and Third Reports on CEDAW." Port Vila.

PEDF (Pacific Enterprise Development Facility). 2003 "Small and Medium Sized Enterprise Business Survey for the Pacific Region." International Finance Corporation. Sydney.

Piau-Lynch, Andonia. 2007 "Vanuatu: Country Profile on Gender." Japan International Cooperation Agency, Tokyo.

Pitt, M., and S. Khandker. 1998. "The Impact of Group-Based Credit Programs on Poor Households in Bangladesh: Does the Gender of Participants Matter?" *Journal of Political Economy* 106.

Reserve Bank of Vanuatu. 2007. "Quarterly Economic Review." Port Vila.

Schultz, T. Paul. 2002. "Why Governments Should Invest More to Educate Girls." *World Development* 30 (2): 207–25.

Secretariat of the Pacific Community. 2005. "Revised Pacific Platform for Action on Advancement of Women and Gender Equality: 2005 to 2015. A Regional Charter." New Caledonia.

Tarisesei, Jean. 1998. "Today Is Not the Same as Yesterday, and Tomorrow It Will Be Different Again: Kastom in Ambae, Vanuatu," in *Women and Governance: From the Grassroots in Melanesia*, ed. B. Douglas. Sorrento, Victoria: State, Society and Governance in Melanesia.

UNDP (United Nations Development Programme). 2007. "Financial Services Assessment: Kiribatu, Tuvalu, Samoa, Solomon Islands, Vanuatu." New York.

Vanuatu National Provident Fund. *Annual Report, 2007*. Port Vila.

Vanuatu Rural Development and Training Centers Association. 2007. "Vanuatu NGO Shadow Report on the Implementation of CEDAW." Port Vila.

Vanuatu Statistics Office. 2000. "Labor Market Survey Report." Port Vila.

———. 2006. "The Vanuatu Poverty Report Card " Port Vila.

———. 2007. "2006 Agriculture Census." Port Vila.

———. 2008. "Analysis of the 2006 Household Income and Expenditure Survey and a Report on the Estimation of Basic Needs Poverty Lines, and the Incidence and Characteristics of Poverty in Vanuatu." Port Vila.

Verschoor and others. 2006. *Women's Economic Empowerment: Gender and Growth: Literature Review and Synthesis*. Report to DfID, Overseas Development Group, University of East Anglia. Cited in Gender and Growth: DFID practice paper, Growth Team Briefing Note 5, March 2007.

World Bank. 2001. *Engendering Development: Through Gender Equality in Rights, Resources, and Voice*. Washington, DC: World Bank.

———. 2007. *Doing Business in 2008*. World Bank, Washington, DC.

———. 2008. *Doing Business in 2009*. Washington, DC. http://www.doingbusiness. org.

Index

Boxes, figures, maps, notes, and tables are indicated by b, f, m, n, and t, respectively.

enforcement of contracts. *See* contract enforcement
England and Wales, 9, 28, 36, 41
Enterprise Challenge Fund, AusAID, 58
EPA (European Partnership Agreement), 80
Epi, 21*b*, 46, 70
equal pay requirements, 71
Erromango, 85*b*
ESCAP (United Nations Economic and Social Commission for Asia and the Pacific), 5
Espiritu Santo, 28
European Partnership Agreement (EPA), 80

F

fair trade certification programs, 83–86, 84–85*b*
Fairtrade Labelling Organizations International (FLO), 85
Family Protection Order Bill, 8, 22–23
Family Protection Unit, 23
family responsibilities of women in Vanuatu, xi, 7, 20, 67, 69, 91
farming. *See* agriculture
female economic participation in Vanuatu. *See* Vanuatu, economic participation of women in
FIAS (Foreign Investment Advisory Service), xi–xii, 35
FICs (Forum Island Countries), 80–81, 83
Fiji
    in *Doing Business* rankings, 6*f*
    financing and credit, 59
    international conventions, application of, 32
    land ownership and registration, 46*f*
    trading across borders, 59, 80, 82*f*, 87*n*4
Financial Institutions Act, 58
financing and credit, 11.53–61
    business skills and financial literacy, 15*t*, 60
    collateral, 58–59
    commercial finance, 58–60
    difficulty of access to, 53–55, 54*f*
    Doing Business rankings, Vanuatu in, 7*t*, 54, 59*t*
    focus groups on, 54–55, 90–91
    legal framework, 58–59
    microfinancing, 8, 55–57, 56–57*b*

offshore financial services in Vanuatu, 25, 53
rating agencies, lack of, 59–60
recommended reforms, 11, 15–16*t*, 60–61
fishing, 79–80
FLO (Fairtrade Labelling Organizations International), 85
focus group discussions with women entrepreneurs, 54–55, 89–92
Foreign Investment Advisory Service (FIAS), xi–xii, 35
formal employment sector, 67–72, 69*f*
Forum Island Countries (FICs), 80–81, 83
France, 28, 58
free trade, 80–83

G

gender and economic participation in Vanuatu. *See* Vanuatu, economic participation of women in
gender discrimination, laws regarding, 29–32, 30*b*, 73
gender equality in Vanuatu, concepts of, 19–21, 29–32, 30*b*
Gender Group, World Bank, ix, xi–xii
gender-segregated data, lack of, 13*t*, 26, 27*t*
government employment of women, 72
Grameen Bank, 56*b*, 87*n*6
Great Britain, 9, 28, 36, 41

H

handicrafts, 77–79, 84–85*b*
haosgels (domestic workers), women as, 70
Hong Kong, China, 64*f*

I

IFC (International Finance Corporation), ix, xi–xii, 7–8, 11, 66
ILO (International Labour Organization), 70, 71
informal employment sector, 68, 69*t*
International Finance Corporation (IFC), ix, xi–xii, 7–8, 11, 66
International Labour Organization (ILO), 70, 71
international trade. *See* trading across borders

J

justice. *See* legal framework

ECO-AUDIT
Environmental Benefits Statement

The World Bank is committed to preserving endangered forests and natural resources. The Office of the Publisher has chosen to print **Women in Vanuatu** on recycled paper with 30 percent post-consumer waste, in accordance with the recommended standards for paper usage set by the Green Press Initiative, a nonprofit program supporting publishers in using fiber that is not sourced from endangered forests. For more information, visit www.greenpressinitiative.org.

Saved:
- 4 trees
- 3 million BTUs of total energy
- 381 lbs. of CO_2 equivalent of greenhouse gases
- 1,583 gallons of waste water
- 203 lbs. of solid waste

green
press
INITIATIVE